Greening Household Behaviour

THE ROLE OF PUBLIC POLICY

OECD

This work is published on the responsibility of the Secretary-General of the OECD. The opinions expressed and arguments employed herein do not necessarily reflect the official views of the Organisation or of the governments of its member countries.

Please cite this publication as:
OECD (2011), *Greening Household Behaviour: The Role of Public Policy*, OECD Publishing.
http://dx.doi.org/10.1787/9789264096875-en

ISBN 978-92-64-06362-4 (print)
ISBN 978-92-64-09687-5 (PDF)

The statistical data for Israel are supplied by and under the responsibility of the relevant Israeli authorities. The use of such data by the OECD is without prejudice to the status of the Golan Heights, East Jerusalem and Israeli settlements in the West Bank under the terms of international law.

Corrigenda to OECD publications may be found on line at: *www.oecd.org/publishing/corrigenda*.

Foreword

*H*ousehold consumption patterns and behaviour have a profound effect on stocks of natural resources and the quality of the environment. The importance of taking the "demand side" into account is a key lesson arising from the OECD's Green Growth Strategy (www.oecd.org/greengrowth). OECD governments have introduced a wide variety of measures to encourage people to take environmental impacts into account in their purchases and practices. Yet, the consequences of such policy measures on household decision-making are not always well understood.

In an effort to fill this gap, a survey of 10 000 households across the OECD was implemented. The study focuses on five areas: households' water use, energy use, personal transport choices, organic food consumption, and waste generation and recycling. Analysis of the responses offers insight into the market, demographic and policy factors that actually influence people's environmental behaviour and consumption patterns.

Not surprisingly, it is found that relative prices of "clean" and "dirty" options matter. However, in many cases this will not be enough, and complementary measures will have to be introduced. These include: information-based measures which allow households to express their preferences for environmental quality; investment in infrastructure which allows them to choose "greener" options at reasonable cost and convenience; and, supporting policy measures which help overcome barriers and failures in the market which discourage environmentally-preferable behaviour and consumption.

Perhaps the most important lesson from the study is that there is wide variation across households in terms of underlying environmental norms. Often their effect on actual decision-making often differs from what one would expect. An improved understanding of how preferences for environmental quality are formed and how they interact with policy design is necessary to addressing the environmental challenges we face. This book is a first and important step in casting light on these issues.

Simon Upton
OECD, Director of Environment

Acknowledgements

This book is a product of the Working Party on National Environmental Policies (now known as the Working Party on Integrating Environmental and Economic Policies), a group under the OECD's Environmental Policy Committee (EPOC). The delegates provided valuable direction, comments and suggestions.

The OECD work on Environmental Policy and Household Behaviour benefited from the support of a number of contributors including: the Australian Department of the Environment and Water Resources; Environment Canada; the Dutch Ministry of Housing, Spatial Planning and the Environment (VROM); the German Federal Ministry for the Environment, Nature Conservation and Nuclear Safety; the French Ministry for Ecology and Sustainable Development (MEEDDM); the Czech Ministry of the Environment; the Mexican Ministry of the Environment and Natural Resources (SEMARNAT); the Korean Ministry of Environment; the Norwegian Ministry of the Environment; the Region Emilia Romagna in Italy and the Swedish Energy Agency (STEM). The Secretariat gratefully acknowledges the financial contributions which allowed it to carry out this work.

The Secretariat is also grateful to the Advisory Committee which was set up to help inform the project and to ensure the political relevance of the outcome of this work. The Committee members from countries participating in the survey, OECD Directorates working in related areas, the International Energy Agency (IEA) and academy met regularly to provide guidance on the questionnaire design and the survey implementation, and to discuss the results.

This project was co-ordinated by the OECD. A consortium of research teams prepared the technical reports which served as the main inputs to the different chapters in this publication. The research team leaders were: Stefano Boccaletti (Catholic University of Piacenza, Italy), Ida Ferrara (York University, Canada), Quentin Grafton (The Australian National University), Alejandro Guevara-Sanguines (Universidad Iberoamericana, Mexico), Kwang-yim Kim (Korean Environment Institute), Bengt Kriström (SLU University, Sweden), Katrin Millock (CNRS – University Panthéon-Sorbonne, France) and Milan Ščasný (Charles University, the Czech Republic). In addition, Hanne Marit Dalen and Bente Halvorsen (Statistics Norway) prepared a cross-cutting report focussing on gender difference. The full technical reports are available at: http://dx.doi.org/10.1787/9789264096875-en and www.oecd.org/environment/households/greeningbehaviour.

This publication has been prepared by Ysé Serret-Itzicsohn and Nick Johnstone, in close co-operation with Fleur Watson, Ivan Haščič and Anthony Cox of the OECD's Environment Directorate.

The assistance of Eavan Coyle in the editing and preparation of the manuscript is greatefully acknowledged.

Table of Contents

Tables

Figures

List of acronyms

CO_2	Carbon dioxide
EEA	European Environment Agency
EPIC	Environmental Policy and Individual Change
GHG	Greenhouse Gas
IEA	International Energy Agency
LESA	Landlord's Energy Saving Allowance
LPG	Liquefied Petroleum Gas
NGO	Non-Governmental Organization
O_3	Ozone
PM	Particulate Matter
UNFCCC	United Nations Framework Convention on Climate Change
VAT	Value Added Tax
VOCs	Volatile Organic Compounds
WTP	Willingness-to-pay

Executive Summary

Household consumption patterns and behaviour have a profound effect on stocks of natural resources and the quality of the environment. As a consequence, governments have introduced a wide variety of measures to encourage people to take environmental impacts into account in their purchases and practices. Recent initiatives include the phasing out of incandescent light bulbs, the introduction of energy performance labels for homes, and the provision of tax incentives to purchase alternative-fuelled vehicles.

As governments promote strategies to encourage more environmentally sustainable consumption patterns, this new OECD survey of households offers insight into what really works and what factors affect people's behaviour. The study focuses on **five areas**: households' **water** use, **energy** use, personal **transport** choices, organic **food** consumption, and **waste** generation and recycling.

This publication presents the **main results** arising from the analysis of the survey responses, as well as the policy implications of these findings. It is based on responses from over 10 000 households in ten OECD countries: Australia, Canada, the Czech Republic, France, Italy, Korea, Mexico, the Netherlands, Norway and Sweden.

Providing the right economic incentive is key

The findings confirm the importance of providing the right incentive to **spur behavioural change**. The survey shows that price-based incentives encourage energy and water savings. For instance, households charged for their consumption on a volumetric basis consume approximately 20% less water than those who are not charged. In addition, they are more likely to install water-efficient equipment at home. Similarly, charging households for the mixed waste that they generate increases recycling volumes. Finally, higher fuel costs are found to reduce car ownership and use, confirming results from previous studies.

Moreover, the evidence indicates that the effect of pricing consumption on a volumetric basis is partially informational – providing a signal to households about consumption levels. Indeed, survey responses indicate a **lack of**

knowledge among respondents about their **actual water and electricity consumption** levels if their consumption is not metered at the household level. The mere fact of metering and introducing a price on the use of environment-related resources has an effect on people's decision making, even if the price is very low. This suggests that recent campaigns to provide information to consumers by installing smart meters that display accurate real-time information on energy use in the home will affect household decisions to some extent even at low prices.

In general the results suggest that **introducing price-based measures and changing relative prices** (for electricity, water, fuel or waste disposal services) is necessary if emissions are to be reduced and natural resources to be conserved.

Information and education play a significant complementary role

In addition to the significant role played by price-based measures, the survey findings indicate that **"softer" instruments**, based on the provision of information to consumers and on public education, can have a substantial complementary role to induce changes on the demand side. The results obtained indicate that the role of soft policy measures is more significant than earlier assessments of policy instruments have found.

The study pays particular attention to the **role of environmental awareness and households' concern for the environment**, and the impacts these have on decision making. Respondents who express a particular concern for the environment relative to other issues, are more likely to adopt practices and make investments which reduce environmental impacts. For example, environmental awareness is a main driver for water-saving behaviours and reduces the likelihood of owning a car. Concern for the environment also influences demand for energy-efficient appliances and renewable energy, as well as the intensity of waste recycling and decisions to consume organic food. In some cases, the effects may be indirect. For instance, results indicate that concern for solid waste generation has a negative impact on the likelihood of drinking bottled water.

This indicates that an important task for governments may be to bolster information campaigns in order to raise people's environmental awareness and induce behavioural change. Increased awareness of the environmental impacts of consumption choices may **also increase the political acceptability of policies**, facilitating their implementation. Once in place, enforcement costs may also be reduced since the policies are more likely to be seen as justified by households.

In addition to the impact of respondents' awareness and concern for environmental issues, this work emphasises **the role of people's social and environmental norms more generally**. Policies can have an effect on norms, for instance on how we see the environmental good which is to be protected by the government measures. This is illustrated in the case of households' willingness-to-pay for a recycling programme. The results indicate that intrinsic motivations such as a sense of civic duty play a significant role in explaining our recycling efforts. As such, policy makers need to take into account the effect of different policy measures on individuals' underlying norms. Further work on the relationship between norms, policy instruments, and household decision making could be usefully carried out.

Even if consumers are concerned about the environmental impacts of their purchase decisions and have strong pro-environmental norms, they may not have access to the information required to behave accordingly. The findings also stress the usefulness of **providing information on product characteristics** to consumers so that they **can make informed decisions**. Eco-labels need to be clear and comprehensible to work and, as such, measures that encourage ease of identification and understanding of eco-labels are likely to be more effective. Trust in the information provided (and the source of such information) is also central to their effectiveness.

Moreover, **labels** prove to be particularly effective if they identify both "public" and "private" benefits. People are more likely to respond to eco-labels if the environmental benefits co-exist with more direct personal benefits for the consumer, such as reduced energy bills resulting from energy-saving behaviour. The personal health benefits which many respondents associate with the consumption of organic food is another example. Eco-labels **could exploit the potential for such private benefits to a larger extent**, particularly since people's willingness-to-pay for improved environmental quality is often limited.

Operating on the supply side to complement demand side measures

While encouraging household demand for environmental quality through prices and information is key, **the supply of environment-related public services to households** can be an important complement. Measures such as collection services for recyclable materials, the provision of public transportation, or the characteristics of electricity supply, **also clearly matter**. Indeed, the results indicate demand-side measures tend to have a more significant effect on individual behaviour when implemented in combination with investments in environment-related services. For instance, the survey findings confirm that access to public transport has an impact on people's car ownership and how many kilometres they drive. Furthermore, the presence and quality of collection services for recyclables is found to increase recycling participation and intensity, and recycling levels are highest when households have access to door-to-door collection services.

However, it is particularly important to bear in mind the **costs associated** with the provision of such infrastructure. For instance, people's use of public transportation increases significantly if the nearest stop is within five minutes from their residence. Yet, increasing the density of public transport to such an extent can be exceedingly costly. In the area of waste, while a drop-off scheme may be less effective with respect to recycling rates than a door-to-door collection scheme, the latter is likely to be much more costly in terms of service provision.

The survey results indicate governments may have to rely particularly heavily upon **supply side measures in areas where environment-friendly decisions tend to be only weakly driven by household demand**. For instance, people do not appear to be willing to pay very much to use "green" energy, such as wind or solar, rather than conventional energy. This is in line with the findings of previous studies. Indeed, relatively few households are prepared to spend more than 5% above their current electricity bill to use green energy, and almost half of them are not willing to pay anything. Similarly, people do not want to pay a significant price premium to consume organic food products relative to conventional substitutes – generally less than 15%. Overall, 30% of respondents are not willing to spend anything extra for organic food.

This implies that **underlying household demand for environmental quality is unlikely to be sufficient to reach ambitious policy objectives**. Moreover, if there are significant political constraints on the introduction of measures which increase the price of environmentally-damaging behaviour and consumption sufficiently, supply-side measures will have a significant complementary role to play.

Using a mix of instruments to spur behavioural change matters

---

The survey results provide useful insight on conditions under which it may be necessary **to combine instruments in order to increase the efficiency and effectiveness of policies**. The combined use of market-based instruments, information-based policies, and supply-side measures has been discussed above.

In addition, when implementing policy packages targeting household behavioural change, it is essential to keep in mind that households may adjust only after a significant time-lag. Taking into account this delayed responsiveness to price incentives is particularly important when addressing certain environmental concerns where consumption is affected by choices related to investment in capital goods (such as appliances or vehicles), and even by the location and characteristics of their residence. The short-term response may be limited until households adjust their stock of durables and lifestyles, and different measures may provide incentives at different decision points. **Some measures (prices) may have a greater impact on use, while others (labels) may primarily affect investment decisions.** This underlines how instruments can usefully complement each other.

In other cases, it can be efficient for policy makers to introduce complementary policy measures when **market barriers and failures discourage particular types of investments** which mitigate negative environmental impacts. For instance, the benefits of investing in insulation are likely to be much less for tenants than owner-occupiers. In rental properties landlords will have few incentives to undertake such investments since these primarily benefit the tenant through lower energy bills. Similarly, tenants will have little incentive to invest in a property they do not own, particularly if they are not planning to occupy it for a long period of time. Government interventions in the rental market can alleviate such barriers, but must be designed with care.

Recognising variation and targeting specific groups

The survey findings show **significant variation in environmental behaviour** and responsiveness to policy measures across different segments of the population. For instance, responsiveness to waste policies varies depending upon whether households live in rural or urban settings, as well as according to housing type. In many cases, such variation reflects differences in costs and preferences across segments of the population, and is not necessarily directly policy-relevant. In particular, the costs associated with the targeting of policies must be borne in mind when assessing the efficiency of targeting. In some cases, the benefits may not be sufficient to justify the additional cost.

However, the survey findings provided some useful insight in terms of **the identification of the specific groups** which information and promotion campaigns should target. Demographic and socio-economic characteristics (age, education and others) can be used to define distinct segments of the population for which policies are likely to be most effective. For instance, information campaigns to modify personal transport choices will be most effective if they target those groups which have higher car use: men, the middle-aged, and those with higher incomes and education. Finally, this work underlines the significant complementary role that policies other than environmental can play, such as revenue redistribution measures addressing distributional issues or housing policy.

Moreover, **many environmental policies are likely to have adverse distributional effects** and the survey provides evidence in this regard, particularly with respect to residential water use. Low-income households are likely to be most adversely affected by increases in water charges as they spend proportionately more than twice as much on residential water use than high-income households. When introducing measures to address possible disparities between income groups, policy makers need to ensure that the economic efficiency and environmental effectiveness of the policy remains intact.

Analysis of environmental policy from the demand side is receiving increasing attention from governments, with issues such as the adoption of eco-innovations by households. A next round of the OECD Household Survey will be carried out in 2011 with the objective of identifying changes in people's attitudes and behaviour towards the environment, and also of examining ways to promote green growth and the development of a low-carbon economy.

Chapter 1

Policies, Environmental Norms and Household Characteristics

Projections indicate that households' impacts on the environment are likely to increase in the future. As governments develop environmental policies to promote greener behaviour, the OECD survey offers insight into what affects our decisions and what really works in five areas: water use, energy use, personal transport choices, organic food consumption, and waste generation and recycling. Before turning to the presentation of the main results, this introductory chapter reviews some of the main factors that are likely to have an impact on households' environmental practices and behaviour. The political context is first examined with the wide range of policy measures used by OECD countries to influence decision-making. Particular attention is also paid to the role of environmental attitudes and norms, improving our understanding of how policy makers can choose instruments to improve the effectiveness and efficiency of policies.

1. Why household behaviour matters

Household consumption patterns and behaviour have an impact on natural resource stocks, environmental quality, and climate change. Projections indicate that these impacts are likely to increase by 2030 (OECD, 2008a). One key determinant of household consumption is economic growth, with the relative economic importance of countries such as China and India increasing. Rapid growth in the world population, with a projected global population of over 8.2 billion in 2030, will also be an important driver and with a trend towards an ageing population. Urbanisation and changing lifestyles will also influence the structure of consumption.

Concerns about the environmental impacts of consumption have been raised at the global level by the United Nations since the 1992 Earth Summit. In response to the increasing environmental impact of household consumption, governments have introduced a variety of measures to promote more sustainable patterns. Recent initiatives include the introduction of environmentally-related taxes, the phasing-out of incandescent light bulbs, energy performance standards and labels for homes, carbon dioxide (CO_2) emission labels for cars and financial support to purchase less environmentally damaging vehicles and solar panels.

However, designing policies to influence household behaviour is a challenge for policy makers. The objective of the OECD project on "Household Behaviour and Environmental Policy" is to improve the understanding of the determinants of households' responses to environmental policies in five areas: residential energy use, water consumption, transport choices, organic food consumption, and waste generation and recycling. This will allow for the design of more efficient and effective policies, and the conclusions will serve as an input into the OECD's Green Growth Strategy.

Total residential energy use in OECD countries is expected to increase by an average of 1.4% per year from 2003 to 2030. This increase will be more rapid in non-OECD countries where, according to forecasts, residential energy use will be nearly 30% higher than the OECD total in 2030. Residential energy demand grows with income, as households increase their stock of electrical appliances. This results in a rise in energy consumption overall, despite energy efficiency gains (see OECD, 2008a).

Passenger-kilometres travelled (by rail, air, buses and light-duty vehicles) are projected to expand by 1.6% per year worldwide to 2030. Transport-related greenhouse gas (GHG) emissions are also expected to grow significantly. Improvements in the energy efficiency of transport vehicles will be more than offset by increases in the number of vehicles owned and in average vehicle use (OECD, 2008a).

Current waste management policies have been successful in diverting increasing amounts of valuable materials from landfill for further use, thereby reducing the associated environmental impacts. However, municipal waste generation is still rapidly increasing, in particular in non-OECD countries, and waste management will be a major challenge in the coming decade. The generation of municipal waste is projected to increase by 38% from 2005 to 2030 (1.3% per year) within the OECD region (OECD, 2008a).

Significant water scarcities already exist in some regions of the OECD and in many non-OECD countries. Even though many OECD countries in recent years have successfully reduced water use per capita and in total, it is projected that approximately 47% of the world's population will be living in areas with high water stress by 2030, mostly in non-OECD countries (OECD, 2008a).

A review of existing work in these five areas (OECD 2008b) brought to light the need for commensurable data and more empirical work across countries. To this end, a survey covering these five policy areas (energy, waste, organic food, water and personal transport) was implemented in 2008.[1] Ten countries representing different OECD regions took part in the survey: Australia, Canada, the Czech Republic, France, Italy, Korea, Mexico, the Netherlands, Norway and Sweden. Responses from over 10 000 households were collected.[2] The analysis of the survey data was co-ordinated by the OECD Environment Directorate. The list of research teams with extensive experience involved in the project is provided in Annex C. Initial results were presented at the OECD Conference on "Household Behaviour and Environmental Policy" organised by the Environment Directorate, on 3 and 4 June 2009, in Paris.

The project analyses the responses of households to various types of policy measures implemented by governments. These include economic instruments (such as energy taxation, water pricing structure), labelling and information campaigns, direct regulation (technical standards of appliances), and the provision of environment-related public services (recycling schemes, public transport). Differences in environmental behaviour across individuals and households (income, age, household size, education) are also analysed. And finally, the effect of personal environmental attitudes and norms is also assessed.

The objectives of this book are two-fold:

- to present the main findings of the OECD 2008 Household Survey and cross-country analysis on the determinants of households' environmental behaviour; and

- to summarise the main policy implications of the analytical work in the different areas addressed by the survey.

The publication consists of five thematic chapters covering the following areas:

- Water – investment in water-efficient appliances; adoption of water-saving practices; determinants of water consumption levels; willingness-to-pay for improved water quality.

- Energy – investment in energy-efficient appliances; adoption of energy saving practices; decisions to "source" electricity (directly or indirectly) from renewable energy sources; and willingness-to-pay for renewable energy.

- Waste – solid waste generation; recycling efforts (distinguished by material); waste prevention; willingness-to-pay for a recycling service.

- Personal transport – transport mode choice; use of public transport and cycling; vehicle ownership.

- Organic food – consumption levels of organic food (distinguished by food type); willingness-to-pay for organic food.

Finally, the book concludes by providing policy recommendations for the design of effective and efficient policies targeting households.

Before turning to the chapters that summarise the main results, it is important to enumerate some of the main factors that are likely to affect households' environment-related practices and decisions.

2. The environmental policy context

OECD governments use a wide range of policy measures to influence households' decision making in the five areas of study. These include:

- taxes and charges (*e.g.* for fuel);
- subsidies (*e.g.* grants for insulation);
- direct regulation (*e.g.* appliance standards);
- information-based measures (*e.g.* eco-labels); and
- provision of infrastructure (*e.g.* cycle paths).

Table 1.1 provides a summary of examples of policy types for waste, energy, water and transport. In the case of organic agriculture most policy measures are targeted on the supply side. The only measures which are targeted directly on the household are labels. Some of the policy questions examined in the survey in the five areas covered are listed in Annex D.

Table 1.1. **Examples of policy types**

	Waste	Energy	Water	Transport
Information-based measures	Label indicating manufactured from recycled materials.	Energy efficiency label for appliances.	Water efficiency label for washing machines.	CO_2 label for cars.
Taxes	Unit-based waste fee.	CO_2 tax on fuel/ electricity use.	Water charging.	Fuel taxes.
Grants/subsidies	Refund for recyclable bottles.	Grants for installation of solar panels.	Reduced VAT for water-efficient appliances.	Reduced sales tax on alternative-fuelled vehicles.
Performance standards	Minimum recycled content standard.	Minimum thermal efficiency standards for new dwellings.	Minimum water efficiency standard for dishwashers.	Maximum sulphur content in diesel.
Technology standards	Ban on presence of toxics in certain products.	Mandated double-glazing of windows.	Mandated use of dual-flush toilets in new buildings.	Mandated use of catalytic converters.
Supply/access measures	Collection of recyclables.	Option to be supplied with renewable energy.	Not applicable.	Public cycle lanes.

Economic instruments, such as environmentally-related taxes,[3] are often advocated to be the most cost-effective manner to meet environmental objectives. Taxes have a direct effect on relative prices and will provide incentives for polluters and resource users to reflect environmental impacts in their decisions (in other words to internalise externalities). Their relative efficiency will depend very much on the extent to which the tax can be levied directly on the pollutant or resource input, rather than on some proxy for the pollutant. While it is preferable to target the externality directly, this may not be possible at reasonable administrative cost (see Eskeland and Devajaran, 1996 for a discussion).

In some sense subsidies – such as those for alternative-fuelled vehicles or less environmentally damaging household appliances – will have a similar effect as environmentally-related taxes on relative prices, and thus will encourage a change to less polluting alternatives. However, their effects will differ from taxes since subsidising the consumption of a less environmentally damaging good or input will result in increased consumption overall. The importance of this effect will depend on the relative price and income elasticities. Perhaps more importantly, it can be difficult to target subsidies efficiently, whether at the level of either the good (efficient appliances) or the recipient (insulation programmes) (see Wirl and Orasch, 1998).

Direct regulation – such as performance standards or technology standards – are certainly the most widely-used policy affecting household decisions in OECD countries. Standards on the energy efficiency of appliances or cars are particularly common. Outright bans (for example on disposal of some products) are also widely used. Such measures can be quite effective, constraining the behaviour of consumers in a manner which reduces environmental impacts. However, in some cases direct regulation may create rigidities that limit their environmental effectiveness and/or their economic efficiency. Different consumers with different demand and market conditions are not able to trade off product attributes or behavioural choices in a manner that reflects their underlying preferences. This results in greater overall social cost.

Policy makers can also rely on product labelling and public information campaigns. These can fulfil two roles: inform households of the general impacts of their consumption patterns on the environment; and provide information on the environmental impacts of specific products (eco-labels). Assuming that there is an underlying demand for environmental quality, this will affect the choices made by households in the market. Such measures are generally used as complements to other instruments (Newell *et al.*, 1999). However, trust in the source of the information is important, as are other factors such as ease of recognition and understanding.

And finally, policy makers can increase households' access to goods or services that facilitate their ability to adopt less environmentally damaging practices. This could include areas in which the government plays a direct role as "service provider" (as in the case of cycle paths), or a more indirect role as regulator (when making "green" energy).[4] Other aspects of supply, such as direct regulation of the characteristics of supply (support for organic agriculture, for instance) are beyond the scope of this study.

In the different thematic areas covered by the survey, respondents were asked to indicate whether they were subject to specific policy measures. There is variation across countries. For instance, the reported extent to which households face "marginal" incentives to reduce their environmental impacts varies from one country and thematic area to another. While 80% to 90% of households are charged on a per-unit basis for electricity consumption, relatively few houses face unit waste charges (by volume or weight). Moreover, there is much greater variation across countries in the case of waste charging – from almost 80% in Korea to less than 30% in Mexico and Italy. Water charging is in between, with water-rich countries (Canada, Sweden and Norway) having the lowest percentages (see Figure 1.1).

With respect to information-based charges, respondents were shown visual images of eco-labels which were in place in their country. They had to indicate if they recognised these labels, and if they used the information these provided in their consumption choices. Figure 1.2 presents the responses in the areas of organic food and energy efficiency. In the first case, respondents in different countries were shown either one or two labels, while in the latter case they were presented with one to three labels.

Figure 1.1. **Use of unit charging for "environmental" services**

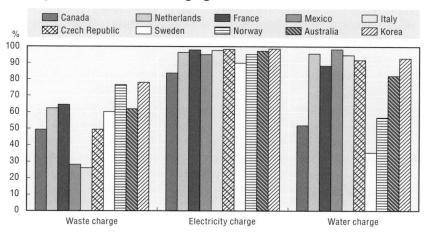

Source: OECD Project on Household Behaviour and Environmental Policy.

Figure 1.2. **Recognition and use of "information-based" measures**
Organic food and energy efficiency

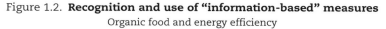

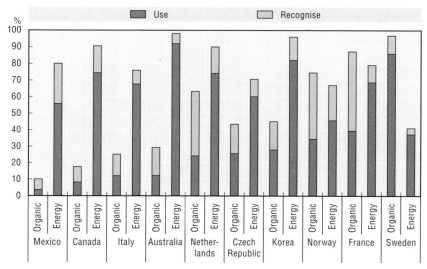

Source: OECD Project on Household Behaviour and Environmental Policy.

Generally, respondents were more likely to recognise and use energy efficiency labels. However, there is variation across countries. In Australia there is high recognition and use of energy efficiency labels and low recognition and use of organic food labels. Swedish respondents reported the opposite. The gap between recognition and use is very small in Sweden and large in Norway, France and the Netherlands (particularly for organic food labels).

Variation in reported use of government measures to give households the option to adopt less environment-intensive practices is presented in Figure 1.3. Three types of measures are presented: ability to explicitly select renewable energy as part of the household's electricity mix; access to public transport within 15 minutes from home; and the availability of door-to-door collection services for wastepaper and cardboard. Giving consumers the option to source their electricity from "renewable" sources seems to be widespread in the Netherlands, particularly in light of the relatively low level of renewables in the fuel mix. Korea, Australia and Sweden also have relatively high reported rates.

Figure 1.3. **Improving access to "environment-related" services**

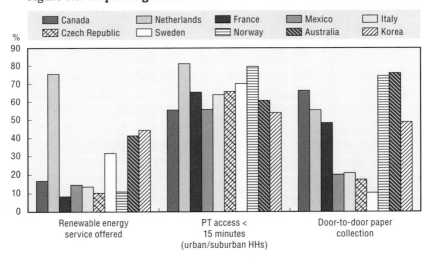

Source: OECD Project on Household Behaviour and Environmental Policy.

Urban and suburban households in the Netherlands and Norway are more likely to live within 15 minutes from a public transport stop or station. Canada, Mexico and Korea have the lowest percentage of households for which this is true. Door-to-door paper collection is common in Australia and Norway, and rare in Mexico, Italy, the Czech Republic and Sweden. However, the percentages are quite different for other materials (see Chapter 4).

Data on government provision of financial support were only obtained from those households that actually made investments in the different areas. In Figure 1.4 these data are presented for dual-flush toilets, water-restrictor

Figure 1.4. **Providing grants (percentage of households having invested who received financial support)**

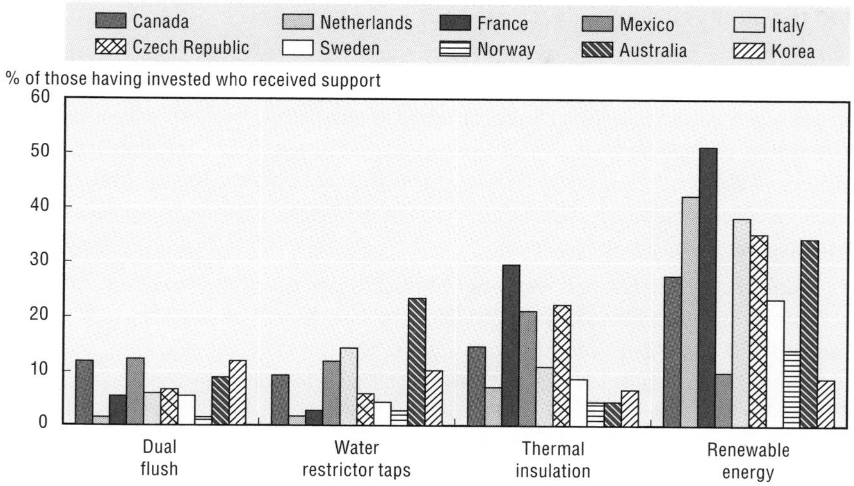

Source: OECD Project on Household Behaviour and Environmental Policy.

taps, thermal insulation and renewable energy. Over 50% of households that had invested in solar panels or residential wind turbines in France had received support for the investments. In Mexico and Korea the figure is less than 10%.

For thermal insulation, France also has the highest percentage, although it is less than 30%. For the water-efficiency related investments, the figures are lower. This is certainly due in part to the relative cost of such investments, making explicit programmes of this kind relatively more administratively burdensome. Australian respondents were more likely (over 12%) to say that they received support for their investment in water-restrictor taps. For dual-flush toilets, Korea, Mexico and Canada are the only countries for which more than 10% received support.

The effect that these different policy measures (and others) have on environmental behaviour and investments is reviewed in the thematic chapters which follow.

3. The role of environmental attitudes and norms[5]

As noted in the introductory chapter, one of the distinct contributions of this project is the attention paid to the role of attitudinal characteristics (e.g. environmental concerns, norms and values) in determining environmental practices and behaviour. Such motivations have not been an important element in much of the previous work on household responses to environmental policies. However, some previous studies which have taken norms into account include analyses of energy use,[6] travel mode choices,[7] organic food purchases[8] and recycling activities.[9]

Better understanding of how norms and values affect the environmental behaviour of individuals can provide useful insights to policy makers for choosing (and combining) instruments to improve the effectiveness and efficiency of policies. In the longer term, governments can also influence norms (Nyborg, 2003), particularly through information-based instruments such as communication campaigns; this may also contribute to increasing the political acceptability of policies.

Conversely, there are areas where households' reactions to the introduction of environmental policies might be less pronounced than predicted by models that do not take into account the effects on norms. For example, evidence suggests that households have strong personal motivations to sort waste, and that relying on mandates or economic incentives may undermine such motivations (Frey, 1999; Frey and Oberholtzer-Gee, 1997).

How concerned were the respondents over specific environmental issues? Taken together, respondents in the ten countries surveyed expressed the highest degree of concern over natural resource depletion, air and water pollution, and climate change. Noise and genetically-modified organisms were the areas in which respondents expressed the least concern (see Figure 1.5).

Figure 1.5. **Respondents' degree of concern over selected environmental issues**

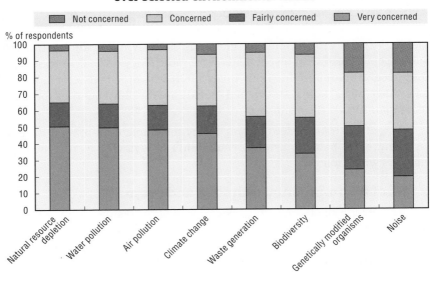

Source: OECD Project on Household Behaviour and Environmental Policy.

At the level of individual countries, respondents in Mexico were those who were most often "very concerned", while respondents in the Netherlands, Norway and Sweden were least often "very concerned". Sweden is the only country where climate change is the issue for which respondents were most likely to say they were very concerned. Noise is cited as being more of a concern in Korea than elsewhere (Figure 1.6).

Figure 1.6. **Percentage of respondents who are "very concerned" over a given environmental issue**

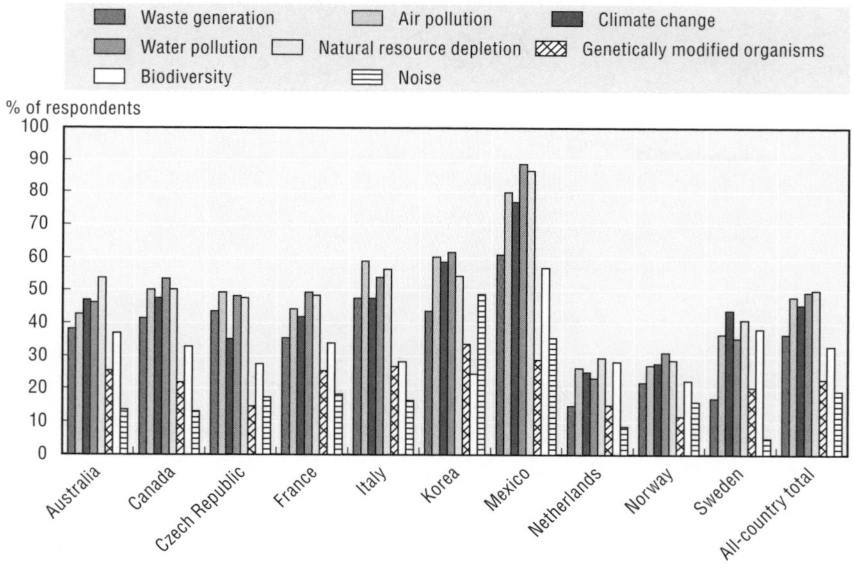

Source: OECD Project on Household Behaviour and Environmental Policy.

In the second section of the questionnaire, five general statements relate to environmental attitudes. Respondents were asked to indicate whether they strongly disagree (2), disagree (1), have no opinion (0), agree (–1), or strongly agree (–2). An environmental attitude index was constructed, with values ranging from –2 to +2, a higher value of the index indicating more pro-environmental values/attitudes.

The figures below present these data, first for European countries and then for the other countries. Amongst the European countries, the Czech distribution is further to the right indicating a stronger reported attitude toward environmental concerns. The Italy distribution is to the left of the other European countries. Amongst the other countries, the Canadian and

Figure 1.7. **Environmental attitude by country (percentage of respondents)**

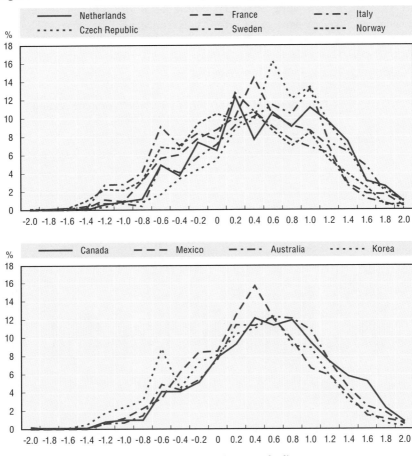

Source: OECD Project on Household Behaviour and Environmental Policy.

Australian distributions are to the right of those of Mexico and Korea. (Evidence on the relationship between the index and demographic and socio-economic factors is presented in the Annex 1.A1 to this chapter.)

One of the individual questions underlying this index was included in order to elicit information on respondents' sense of personal responsibility for environmental concerns. In Figure 1.8 country-level data on the extent to which respondents disagreed (or strongly disagreed) with the statement that "individuals/households can contribute to a better environment" are presented.

Relatively few respondents disagreed with this statement. However, it is interesting to note that the Dutch and Australian respondents are (with the Norwegians) the most likely to disagree with this statement. They are, however,

Figure 1.8. **Percentage of households who disagree with the statement that each individual/household can contribute to a better environment**

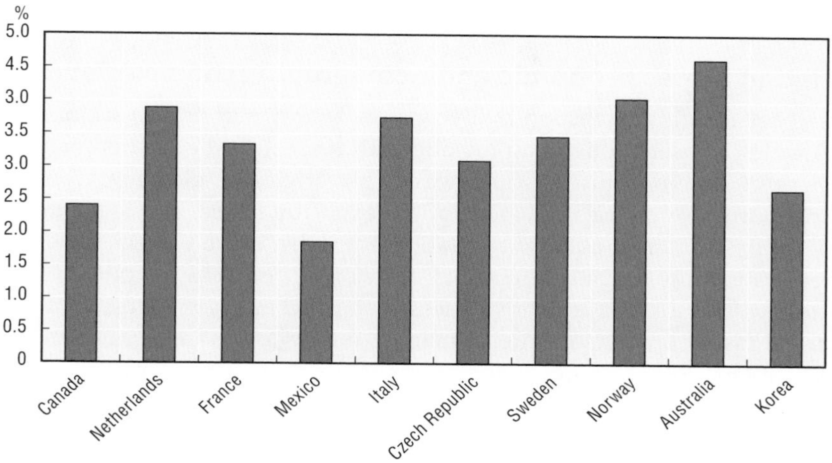

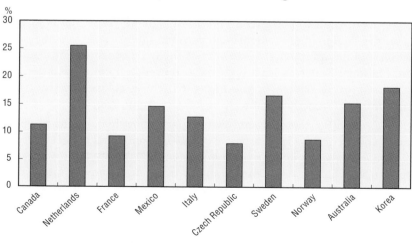

Source: OECD Project on Household Behaviour and Environmental Policy.

the most likely to be "members of (or contributors to) an environmental organisation" (see Figure 1.9). This underscores the importance of taking into account attitudes toward environmental concerns, and how respondents feel they can be best addressed, when assessing the determinants of environmental practices. Perhaps more importantly, it also underscores the need in empirical

Figure 1.9. **Percentage of respondents who are members of (or contributors to) an environmental organisation**

Source: OECD Project on Household Behaviour and Environmental Policy.

analyses to take into account cultural factors which may affect how individuals respond to a given question – i.e. through the inclusion of control variables for country of residence.

4. Variation across economic and demographic characteristics

There is little question that economic factors play an important role in affecting household decision making with respect to the environment. The price of the good in question (water, electricity) is clearly paramount. Environmental policies influence prices explicitly (taxes, subsidies, tradable permits, etc.) or implicitly (regulations). However, even in the absence of environmental policies, household decisions in environmentally-sensitive areas will be affected by relative prices. Rising fuel prices will affect household decisions to purchase a fuel-efficient vehicle (or change travel modes), whether or not the source of the price change arises from a fuel tax, scarcity of the resource, or the existence of an oil cartel.

By increasing consumption levels, higher income can clearly have negative implications for environmental pressures in aggregate. However, the relationship is not necessarily negative. For instance, household income can positively affect the extent to which households take environmental factors into account in their decision making in all of these five areas. This can arise both directly and indirectly. On the one hand, depending upon the income-elasticity of demand for environmental quality, richer households will be more or less likely to pay a premium for environmental factors when purchasing different goods and services. While it is generally found that the income-elasticity of demand for environmental quality is positive, it is unclear whether it is greater than unity, and it may vary greatly depending upon the "good" in question.[10]

Respondents to the survey were requested to rank a set of six issues in terms of their importance to them. In general, respondents in the ten countries tend to rank economic and personal safety issues as a high priority, social and environmental issues are of medium concern, and health and international issues as least important. However, there is variation across income groups. Those in the highest income classes tended to rank environmental concerns relatively higher (see Figure 1.10).

On the other hand, greater income may allow households to purchase goods and services which have more or less environmental impact, irrespective of their underlying preferences for environmental quality. For instance, many appliances which save on energy and/or water are relatively more costly at the outset, but result in lower operating costs over their lifetime. Conversely, the "cost" of taking the time to sort recyclables may be much greater for high-income households. All of these examples illustrate the fact that there are often a mixture of private (finance, health, convenience, etc.) and public (environmental quality) factors at play in the decisions addressed in this report.

Figure 1.10. **Percentage of respondents ranking environmental concerns in the top 3 out of 6 concerns**

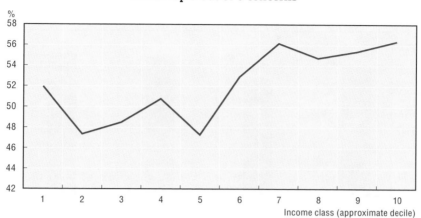

Income class (approximate decile)

Source: OECD Project on Household Behaviour and Environmental Policy.

In addition, environmental behaviour and consumption patterns may vary across household demographic factors such as gender, educational status, household size and composition, location of residence, etc. An assessment of the role of these factors is necessary in order to determine the effect of policy variables on environment-related behaviour and practices in specific areas. For instance, the effect of recycling programmes can vary significantly depending upon household composition and occupation status. In addition, tenants may be less likely to undertake costly investments with positive environmental consequences than owner-occupiers whose benefits are only realised over the long term. It may be necessary to design policies with this in mind.

The demographic characteristics considered include the age and gender of the respondent, household size, marital status, and the presence of children in the household. In many cases there are clear differences between apparent demand for environmental quality. For example, Figure 1.11 presents data on the percentage of respondents with and without children who have a positive willingness-to-pay for a recycling service, renewable energy, and water quality. While such relationships may be illustrative, the thematic chapters report on formal empirical analysis of the relative importance of such factors.

In some cases, the existence of environmental externalities may not be the only source of market inefficiency. Other sources of market barriers and failures in consumer markets include: information asymmetries; capital market failures; and split incentives.[11] Particular groups may be particularly subject to such barriers and failures and when this is the case, policy makers

Figure 1.11. **Willingness-to-pay for different environmental "goods"**

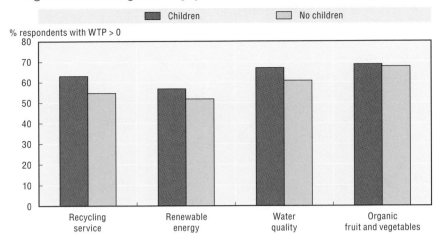

Source: OECD Project on Household Behaviour and Environmental Policy.

may need to use complementary measures to remove other failures in addition to the instruments more directly targeting the environmental externality. As such, some of these measures need to be targeted at specific household groups to improve the effectiveness and efficiency of the policy.

For instance, some households (*e.g.* low-income households) may face constraints to access the credit market, preventing them from making investments in environmentally preferable goods (*e.g.* alternative fuel vehicles, water/energy efficient equipments) which would appear to be cost-effective for them to undertake. In general, it is found that households would have to discount the benefits of reduced future expenditures by as much as 20% *per annum* in order to explain why they choose less energy-efficient durables in favour of more efficient alternatives.[12] If this is not a true reflection of underlying preferences, policy makers may need to adopt complementary measures to address these barriers in the capital market. These measures include grants or preferential loans targeted at vulnerable households.

In addition, some households may face few incentives to invest in environmentally preferable goods or to adopt environmental behaviour. For instance, the landlord has little incentive to choose the most water/energy-efficient equipment (such as space heaters and lighting systems) and/or to invest in insulation, when the tenant benefits from these choices through reduced energy/water bills (see Sorrell, 2004). Governments may need to introduce targeted measures to address this source of market failure (see Figure 1.12).

Figure 1.12. **Percentage of owner-occupiers and tenants having undertaken specific investments**

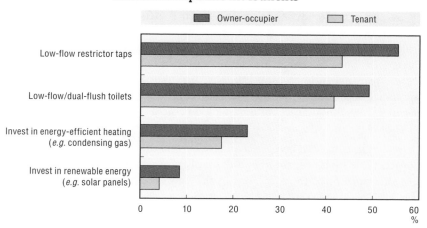

Source: OECD Project on Household Behaviour and Environmental Policy.

There are, therefore, cases in which policies should be targeted at (or designed for) specific groups. However, such targeting may not be costless. In particular, targeting measures at specific groups may entail important administrative costs that need to be taken into account by policy makers.

5. Conclusion

The results of more formal analyses of the relationship between policy measures, environmental attitudes and norms, and household socio-economic characteristics are summarised in the following chapters. The analyses cover actual purchase decisions (e.g. energy-efficient appliances), behaviour (e.g. water-saving practices), and willingness-to-pay for goods which are perceived to yield environmental benefits (e.g. organic agriculture). These factors may play very different roles in the different areas covered.

Part of the reason for this is due to the fact that in all of the decisions assessed, a complex mixture of "public" and "private" considerations enter into households' decision-making processes, and the relative importance of private and public motivations in specific decisions varies from one area to the other. For instance, the purchase of energy-efficient and water-efficient appliances may reduce pressure on the environment (public benefits) and expenditures on water and energy use (private benefit). Purchasing a fuel-efficient car may as well reduce emissions of greenhouse gases (public benefits) and reduce vehicle operating costs (private benefits). Similarly, purchasing organic food products may result in lower use of pesticides (public benefits) and improved personal health (private benefits).

In addition, there is variation in the nature of the decisions and choices which households make. For instance the determinants of whether or not to own a car may differ from the factors affecting car use, and better understanding of these different mechanisms can matter when it comes to influencing household decision-making processes. In a similar way, the decision about whether or not to be equipped with a certain appliance may differ from decisions which relate to frequency and nature of use of the appliance. More subtly, decisions to recycle or to consume organic food may be distinct from the quantity of organic food consumed in the household or the level of recycling effort.

The time horizon involved can also be very different. In the case of energy demand, for instance, there is a dynamic component that clearly separates the short run form the long run. In the short run, the capital stock is fixed (*e.g.* heating system installed) and, therefore, the short-term response to a measure like price changes may be smaller than the long-term response. In a similar way, there are sharp differences in the possible types of adjustment of households to policies related to personal transport choices in the short run and long run. For instance, individuals may decide to adapt to the increased cost of motoring by changing to a more fuel-efficient vehicle or even moving to another place of residence to facilitate access to public transport. An important consideration when designing policies targeted at households is that in some areas a significant time lag exists for households to adjust.

Such differences should be borne in mind when interpreting the results presented in the chapters which follow. The implications for policy design are discussed in the concluding section of each chapter, as well as in the concluding chapter of the book.

Notes

1. For a description of the survey methodology and sample see Annex A.

2. The full OECD survey questionnaire is provided in Annex B (Canadian English version).

3. Tradable permits have similar characteristics, but there are few cases which target households directly.

4. See Goodwin (1995) for a discussion in the transport context.

5. This section (and the accompanying Annex 1.A1) is based on work undertaken by Ivan Haščič (OECD Secretariat).

6. See Lutzenheiser (1993). Viklund (2002) provides a review of the literature.

7. See Bamberg and Schmidt (2003) and Heath and Gifford (2002).

8. See Grunert and Juhl (1995) and Tanner and Kast (2003).

9. See Berglund and Matti (2006) and Thørgersen (2003).

10. With an income elasticity of demand greater than unity "demand" for improved environmental quality would increase more than proportionately with income. See Pearce (2006) for a review of the evidence.

11. Cases such as where owner-occupiers are more likely to make investments than tenants in cases where benefits are incurred over a period of time.

12. See OECD (2002) for a review of the literature.

References

Eskeland, G. and S. Devarajan (1996), *Taxing Bads by Taxing Goods: Pollution Control with Presumptive Charges*, World Bank, Washington DC.

Frey, B.S. (1999), "Morality and Rationality in Environmental Policy", *Journal of Consumer Policy*, No. 22, pp. 395-417.

Frey, B.S. and F. Oberholzer-Gee (1997), "The Cost of Price Incentives: An Empirical Analysis of Motivation Crowding Out", *American Economic Review*, Vol. 87(4), pp. 746-755.

Newell, R., A. Jaffe and R. Stavins (1999), "The Induced Innovation Hypothesis and Energy-Saving Technological Change", *Quarterly Journal of Economics*, Vol. 114, No. 3, pp. 941-75.

Nyborg, K. (2003), "The Impact of Public Policy on Social and Moral Norms: Some Examples", *Journal of Consumer Policy*, Vol. 26(3), pp. 259-277.

OECD (2008a), *Environmental Outlook to 2030*, OECD, Paris.

OECD (2008b), *Household Behaviour and the Environment: Reviewing the Evidence*, OECD, Paris.

Sorrell, S. (2004), *The Economics of Energy Efficiency: Barriers to Cost-Effective Investment*, Edeward Elgar.

Wirl, F. and W. Orasch (1998), "Analysis of United States' Utility Conservation Programs", in *Review of Industrial Organization*, Vol. 13, pp. 467-486.

ANNEX 1.A1

Household Characteristics and Environmental Norms and Attitudes

Analysis of the data were conducted to examine the socio-demographic characteristics, and other factors, for possible correlation with environmental attitudes (as reflected in the index mentioned above), while controlling for cross-country differences in households' purchasing power as well as other unobserved country-specific heterogeneity (fixed effects). It is found that gender (being a female), education (post-secondary), and to a lesser extent urban place of residence, are positively (and at statistically significant levels) correlated with the environmental attitude (Figure 1.A1.1). In addition, certain types of occupation (liberal professions and salaried employees) are also correlated with the index.

Approximately 14% of respondents indicated that they were members of (or financially supported) an environmental organisation. This varies by country with the highest membership rates in the Netherlands (25%) and lowest in Norway and the Czech Republic (8.4% and 8.0%). Figure 1.A1.2 gives odds ratios* summarising results of empirical models estimated. Individuals of older age, having young children, post-secondary education, or higher income are correlated with the likelihood of being a member of an environmental organisation (i.e. have higher odds of being a member than not being one). In addition, the results also suggest that certain types of occupation correlate with membership (e.g. respondents working in liberal professions or as teachers and those working as executives are more likely to be members). The most important finding is that higher levels of education are positively correlated with environmental membership.

Focusing on educational attainment in greater detail, an alternative model was estimated with a more refined disaggregation of the educational

---

* The odds ratio is the ratio of the odds of an event occurring in one group to the odds of it occurring in another group.

Figure 1.A1.1. **Impact of gender, education and place of residence on environmental attitudes**

Estimated elasticity of environmental attitude index to changes in selected (statistically significant) variables

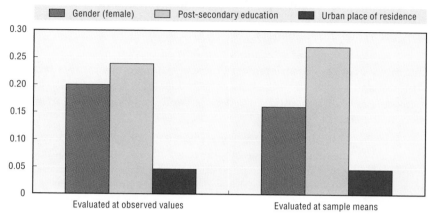

Note: The estimated elasticities are based on: 1) average marginal effects with covariates evaluated at values observed in the sample; and 2) conditional marginal effects with covariates evaluated at mean values of the sample. Estimates based on a panel-data fixed-effects model with explicit controls for socio-demographic characteristics and cross-country differences in purchasing power.

Source: OECD Project on Household Behaviour and Environmental Policy.

Figure 1.A1.2. **Probability of being a member of (or contributor to) an environmental organisation**

Estimated odds ratios

Note: Only selected estimates are reported here. Estimates that are not statistically significant at the 5% level or higher are shown as blank. The estimated odds ratios are derived from a fixed-effects logit model. For the odds ratios to be comparable across covariates, all previously (semi-) continuous variables were transformed into dummy variables around the sample median (this includes age, income and household size).

Source: OECD Project on Household Behaviour and Environmental Policy.

classes. It is found that high school graduates and those having some form of post-secondary education are somewhat more likely to be members compared to respondents who did not graduate from high school (however, these effects are not statistically significant). On the contrary, obtaining a university-level diploma (Bachelor's and above) increases the odds substantially and in a statistically significant manner.

Overall, the level of educational attainment stands out as an important characteristic that is associated with respondents' pro-environmental values, attitudes and behaviour in the data collected. Being a woman is also found to increase pro-environmental attitudes, as well as living in an urban area, though to a lesser extent.

However, the findings vary somewhat depending on the exact issue examined. While gender and age may correlate highly with some of the issues addressed, in other instances composition of the household or income may appear more important. Nevertheless, the overall message that the data deliver is very encouraging – *educational attainment* stands out as an important characteristic that is associated with respondents' pro-environmental values, attitudes and behaviour. This finding is statistically robust and is common to all the issues examined.

Chapter 2

Residential Water Use

Although agriculture and industry represent the bulk of water demand, residential water use accounts for some 10-30% of total consumption in developed countries. This chapter looks at the impacts of policy measures such as water pricing and appliance labelling. It examines the determinants of water-saving behaviour and investment in water-saving appliances and whether having to pay for water according to volume actually reduces consumption. The role of respondent's environmental "norms" is also analysed, suggesting that measures informing households of the environmental implications of excessive water consumption could have a significant complementary part to play. In addition, the question of people's perception of tap water quality is considered in the survey. The chapter presents results on household satisfaction with the quality of tap water and on their motivation to buy bottled water for drinking either for health reasons or for reasons of taste.

1. Introduction

Water scarcity is an environmental problem in many areas of the world. Even countries with abundant water supply face constraints in providing clean drinking water because of water contamination from pollution that raises the costs of water treatment. Although industry and agriculture represent the bulk of water demand, the percentage of residential use in overall water consumption ranges from 10-30% in OECD countries.

Given the high costs of water supply projects, a central element of water policy in OECD countries has been on demand management in order to both reduce the quantity of water used and increase the efficiency of its use. It is essential to design policies that can reduce the demand for water, while providing the same services. Pricing policies have received much attention, particularly since a number of OECD countries mandate full-cost water pricing for residential users.[1] However, tariff structures vary, and this can have at least as important an impact on demand as cost recovery *per se*.

Since most studies find that household water demand is fairly price inelastic, managers of water utilities have sometimes chosen to impose restrictions on water use – *e.g.* hosepipe bans. Mandatory restrictions are commonly applied as a temporary measure in response to severe and unexpected water shortages since it is felt that suddenly imposing higher prices would not generate a sufficient behavioural response. In addition, it is sometimes argued that such a policy places less of a burden on poorer households than a pricing policy.[2]

Other policies target investment in water-efficient equipment purchases. In 2007, California became the first US State to mandate the installation of high efficiency toilets, a requirement that will be introduced in 2010. Several countries have promoted rebate programs for the installation of water-efficient equipment, such as high-efficiency toilets. However, there is little data on adoption of water-efficient equipment, and, apart from Renwick and Archibald (1998), no previous study has examined adoption on a household level.

In addition to analysis of the determinants of water consumption, a better knowledge of consumer preferences with respect to water quality can assist policy makers. With the exception of surveys conducted after specific water contamination incidents (mostly in the US) and a number of studies measuring households' perception of water quality in Canada, there is a scarcity of studies on households' valuation of improved tap water quality in OECD countries.

Public sector investments in water quality services are not the only means at the disposal of households to improve the quality of drinking water. Households can invest in purification systems. Households can also consume bottled water for their drinking needs. Since these are private substitutes for public investments, assessing the factors that encourage the adoption of such private strategies is important for policy design.

The OECD project has provided insight into all of these issues. Drawing upon observations from over 10 000 households in ten OECD countries evidence is presented on the following issues:

- *The determinants of residential water consumption.* This includes a detailed assessment of the impacts of water pricing. It is found that charging for water on a volumetric basis reduces water consumption by 25%. The distributional impacts of water pricing measures are also assessed.

- *The determinants of water-saving behavior.* While water pricing clearly matters, it is found that the environmental "norms" of the respondent are also important. This highlights the importance of informing households of the environmental implications of excessive and wasteful water consumption.

- *The determinants of investment in water-saving residential equipment.* In this case the environmental "norms" of the respondents are important explanations for the investment in water-saving equipment. Above all, what matters the most for investment is home ownership and water charging on a volumetric basis. Attention is also paid to the role of eco-labelling in this case. The results indicate that eco-labelling (in general) complements marginal pricing of water at the point of use.

- *The willingness-to-pay (WTP) for improved water quality services.* While stated WTP is relatively low, in countries where there is significant dissatisfaction with water quality, it is not negligible. Amongst the factors that explain differences in WTP is the level of trust in government authorities.

- *The factors that encourage households to purchase bottled water.* Many of the factors that encourage households to purchase bottled water for usual household consumption are the same as those that explain WTP for improved public water service delivery. However, concern about the negative impacts of solid waste has a very strong negative impact on bottled water consumption.

This chapter is based on a report on "Water Consumption" prepared for the OECD by Quentin Grafton (The Australian National University) and a report on "Household Adoption of Water-Efficient Equipment and Demand for Water Quality" prepared for the OECD by Katrin Millock (CNRS, University Panthéon-Sorbonne, France), Céline Nauges (INRA, Toulouse School of Economics, France), Olivier Beaumais and Anne Briand (CARE-Université de Rouen, France). The full technical reports are available at: *http://dx.doi.org/10.1787/9789264096875-en* and *www.oecd.org/environment/households/greeningbehaviour*.

The chapter presents a summary of the main results arising out of these studies. In the next section, results of the analysis of water consumption are examined. In Section 3, the results of the analysis on water-saving behaviour and investment are summarised. This is followed by a review of respondents' WTP to improved public water service quality, as well as a discussion of the factors which encourage consumption of bottled water. The chapter concludes with a discussion of the main policy conclusions.

2. Determinants of water consumption

1 660 respondents provided details about their water consumption. Figure 2.1 shows the level of consumption in kL per household member per year in the different countries. Mean and median values are provided since the data are skewed, with a small number of households reporting very large consumption levels.[3] Consumption per household member is highest in Canada and Australia. Within Europe, reported consumption for Italy is very high.

Figure 2.1. **Water consumption per household member**

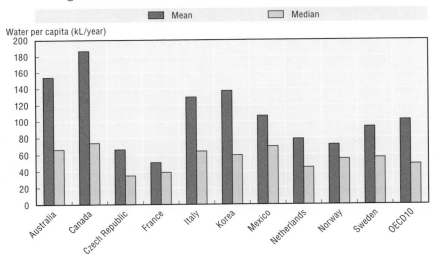

Source: OECD Project on Household Behaviour and Environmental Policy.

Econometric evidence indicates that household characteristics such as the number of people in the household (adults and children) and residence size have a significant and positive impact on water consumption levels. However, the effects are less than proportional, indicating that demographic transitions toward smaller households will likely result in increased water consumption. In addition, higher household income has a statistically significant and positive effect on per capita water consumption. By contrast, there is no evidence that attitudes to the environment or participation in environmental groups or activities, as measured in the survey, have a statistically significant effect on residential water consumption.

From a policy perspective, it is the effect of water pricing which is most relevant. 80 per cent of responding households stated that they were subject to water charges, of which 84 per cent incur water charges based directly on their level of consumption. After controlling for all other potential factors (income, household size, employment, ownership status, residential characteristics, environmental concerns, etc.), it was found that households that face a volumetric charge will, on average, consume about 20% less water than households who do not. For those who are charged volumetrically, an increase in the average water price is likely to lead to a reduction in water consumption.[4] The results indicate that a one per cent increase in the average water price across households would lower residential water use by about 0.56 per cent (see Figure 2.2 for results by country). Water demand of high-income households is less price elastic than the water demand of low and medium-income households.

Figure 2.2. **Price elasticities by country**

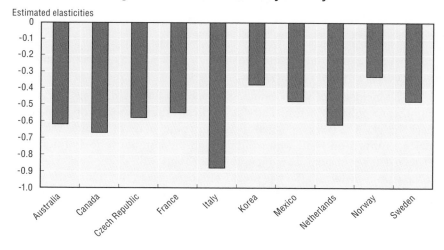

Source: OECD Project on Household Behaviour and Environmental Policy.

A summary of the main results and a comparison with the evidence from other studies is provided in Table 2.1.

A significant percentage of respondents (over 80%) were unable to provide data on household water consumption. This includes households who are charged for water on a volumetric basis. This indicates that many households are unaware of their consumption levels, even when they are

Table 2.1. **Summary of main results and comparison with the literature**

Survey variable	Description	Estimated sign in the OECD10 survey	Expected sign in the literature	Related literature
WTREFEETYPE_UNIT	Dummy variable if households faces volumetric charge	–	–	Dalhusien (2000) (–), Nauges and Thomas (–).
WTRPRICEUNIT	Average water price (EUR/kL)	–	–	Howe and Linaweaver (–), Renwick and Archibald (–).
INCOME_CONT	Household income (EUR)	+	+	Dalhuisen et al. (2000, 2003) (+), Schleich and Hillenbrand (2008), etc.
ADULTS	Number of adults in household	+	+	Hanke and Maré (+), Lyman (+), Gaudin (2006).
CHILDREN_NEW	Number of children	+	+	Lyman (+).
HIGHEDUC	Dummy variable for tertiary education	+	?	
REDSIZE	Residence size (sq. meters)	+	+	Nieswiadomy and Molina (+).
RESDAGE	Residence age (years)	–	+	Lyman (+), Nauges and Thomas (2000) (+).
AREADESC_URBAN	Dummy variable for household living in urban or suburban region	+	–	Domene and Sauri (–), Gaudin (–).
WTRINV_DUAL_1	Dummy variable for having low flush toilet	–	–	Renwick and Archibald (–).

Source: OECD Project on Household Behaviour and Environmental Policy.

charged for it, and underscores the value of information and communication in encouraging water conservation.

The incidence of water charging on poorer households is also an issue of significant policy concern. The data indicate that low-income households (less than EUR 15 000 per annum) spend, as a percentage of income, more than twice as much on their water bill as high-income households (more than EUR 60 000 per annum). Low-income households will, in the absence of any lump sum transfers, suffer the most from increases in the volumetric price of water. This confirms earlier studies that found that the burden of water charges can be up to four times greater for the lowest decile income group when compared to the average burden across all households (OECD, 2003). Full-cost water pricing, coupled with assistance to low-income households in the form of a low or zero fixed fee, or via transfer payments, can help ensure water is used efficiently and allocated equitably across residential consumers.

3. Determinants of water saving behaviours and investments

As noted above, there were a large number of households who were not able to provide information on their level of water consumption. However, they were able to provide information on their water-saving behaviours and investments. Table 2.2 provides information on the reported frequency of undertaking different water-saving behaviours.

Table 2.2. **Summary of responses to water saving behaviours**

	Responses for all households (as a percentage of total responses)				
	Never	Occasionally	Often	Always	Not applicable
Turn off the water while brushing teeth	11.5	19.8	20.1	47.8	0.8
Take shower instead of bath to save water	6.1	8.7	20.3	60.3	4.6
Plug the sink when washing dishes	15.9	17.0	17.2	41.7	8.2
Water the garden in the coolest part of the day	8.6	9.6	15.3	34.0	32.5
Collect rainwater or recycle waste water	32.8	10.8	10.5	19.4	26.5

Source: OECD Project on Household Behaviour and Environmental Policy.

The empirical analyses undertaken indicate that volumetric water charges increase the probability of: 1) turning off the water while brushing teeth; 2) taking a shower instead of a bath; 3) watering the garden in the coolest part of the day; and 4) collecting rainwater and recycling wastewater. In contrast to the estimates of household water consumption, some attitudinal variables, such as having a high level of stated concern for environmental matters, do have a statistically significant effect on the marginal probability of undertaking water saving behaviours.

With respect to capital investments, Figure 2.3 provides information on the share of households in different countries owning various water-efficient appliances and equipment. The level of investment is greatest in Australia and the Netherlands. Overall, Korean households report the lowest rates of ownership. Water-abundant countries such as Norway, Sweden and Canada also report relatively low investment in such equipment.

Households that are charged a volumetric water fee are more likely to have, or to have recently invested in, water-efficient devices than those households charged either no fee or a flat fee for water (see Figure 2.4). For low-volume or dual-flush toilets, 58% of households with a variable water charge have this equipment, compared with 46% for those charged a flat fee and 37% with no water charge at all. The results are similar for water-flow restrictor taps/low-flow showerheads and for water efficient washing machines. The reason for the higher investment in water efficient appliances is clear for those who pay by volume of water consumed.

However, it is less obvious why a greater proportion of households facing a flat fee are more likely to invest in water-efficient appliances, as compared to those households who are not charged for water. This may indicate greater level of water conservation awareness when there is at least partial cost recovery, even if there are no incentives to reduce consumption. This is

Figure 2.3. **Share of households owning water-efficient equipment, by country**

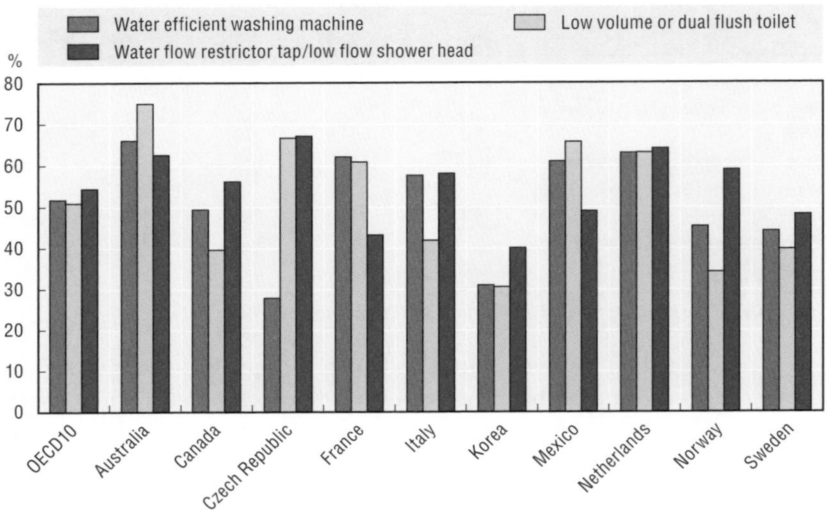

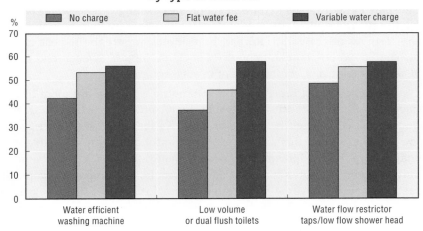

Source: OECD Project on Household Behaviour and Environmental Policy.

Figure 2.4. **Share of households who have water efficient appliances, by type of water fee**

Source: OECD Project on Household Behaviour and Environmental Policy.

indirectly confirmed by the finding that those respondents who were able to report their water consumption levels were more likely to undertake all of the water-saving behaviours and water-efficient equipment investments.

In the empirical analyses undertaken, the size of the household and level of income have positive and significant impacts on take-up of such measures. Ownership status always has a positive impact on adoption of water-efficient equipment, and its marginal impact generally exceeds that of the household size and income. This reflects the importance of "split incentives", i.e. owner-occupiers are more likely to make such investments than tenants. This is in line with theory and previous research results, as well as the results obtained with respect to energy appliances. However, it is interesting that the effect is present even for relatively small investments related to water efficiency – i.e. water restrictor taps. The marginal effect of ownership status on the probability of adoption is approximately 0.06 to 0.10.

Households that pay for their water on a volumetric basis are more likely to adopt indoor water-efficient equipment. The effect relative to households who do not pay for their water at all is similar in magnitude to the effect of being an owner rather than a tenant. If the respondent stated that they took the appropriate environmental label into account in their purchasing decisions, this also increased the probability of adopting indoor water-efficient equipment, particularly for water-efficient washing machines and water flow restrictor taps.

In summary, water charging, ownership status and environmental norms have significant impacts on investment in water-efficient equipment. There are, of course, likely to be significant interactions between these three factors.

4. Willingness-to-pay for improved water quality

In addition to collecting data on water consumption, the OECD survey elicited information on the degree of satisfaction with water quality. Two-thirds of all survey respondents were satisfied with the quality of their tap-water for drinking (Figure 2.5). Of those who expressed dissatisfaction, health concerns were stated approximately twice as frequently as taste concerns. The percentage of respondents who stated that they were satisfied with the quality of their tap for drinking differs significantly by country. Respondents from the Netherlands, Sweden and Norway were almost all satisfied with water quality with 95%, 92% and 90%, respectively, being satisfied. Respondents from Mexico, Korea and Italy were the least satisfied with 79%, 70% and 44% expressing dissatisfaction with water quality. In those countries in which the general level of satisfaction is greatest, taste is a more significant concern than health for those who are dissatisfied. The opposite is true in countries in which the general level of satisfaction is low.

For those households who stated that they were not satisfied with the quality of their tap-water, data were collected on their "willingness-to-pay" for improvements in the public service. A review of the literature indicates that estimated WTP varies from USD 12 to USD 275, and is found to vary with

Figure 2.5. **Household satisfaction with quality of tap-water for drinking, by country**

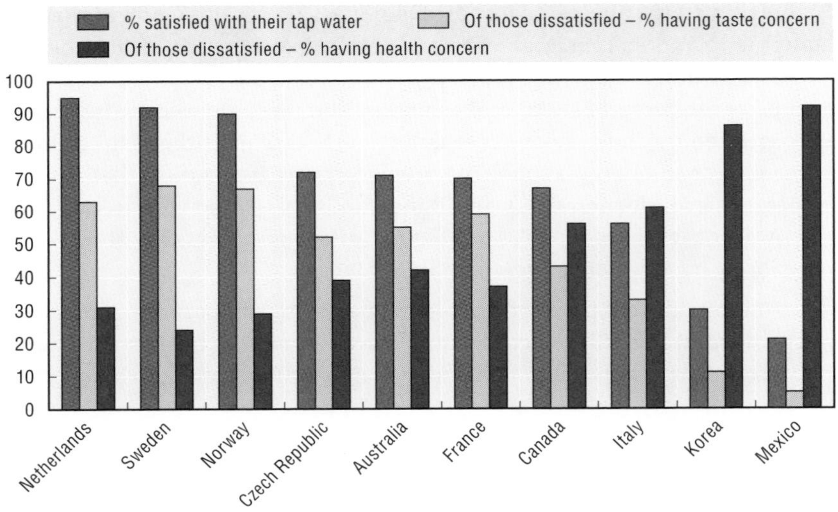

Source: OECD Project on Household Behaviour and Environmental Policy.

households' socio-economic and demographic characteristics, but also with perceived risk and quality (see Table 2.3). Attitudinal characteristics have been less frequently considered, with the exception of Luzar and Cosse (1998), who incorporate the influence of a subjective norm and a measure of the individual's attitudes towards the state of the environment (including water). Both these variables were statistically significant and increased the WTP.

Table 2.3. **Estimates of WTP for improvement in water safety/quality (per household per year)**

Author(s)		Valuation Method	Estimated WTP
Abdalla, Roach and Epp	United States	Averting behaviour	USD 12-USD 26
Abrahams, Hubbell and Jordan	United States	Averting behaviour	USD 47
Dupont	Canada	Averting behaviour	CAD 114-CAD 120
Laughland, Musser, Shortle and Musset	United States	Averting behaviour	USD 46-USD 275
Um, Kwak and Kim	Korea	Averting behaviour	KRW 50-KRW 73
Benson	United States	Contingent valuation	USD 18-USD 48
Kwak, Lee and Russel	Korea	Contingent valuation	KRW 39
Luzar and Cosse	United States	Contingent valuation	USD 77
Powell, Allee and McClintock	United States	Contingent valuation	USD 62
Schultz and Lindsay	United States	Contingent valuation	USD 129
Whitehead	United States	Contingent valuation	USD 19-USD 254

WTP was first estimated on the pooled data and then separately for each of the three countries which had the highest percentage of respondents stating that they were dissatisfied with their tap-water (Italy, Korea and Mexico). The stated WTP is modeled as a function of socio-economic and demographic variables, and attitudinal characteristics of the respondent. We also include the respondent's opinion about tap water, *i.e.* we indicate whether respondents express concerns about health and taste.

The mean and median values for the pooled data (EUR 14) represent about 7.5% of the median annual water bill (see Figure 2.6). At the country level, the median WTP in Italy, Korea and Mexico represents 8.8%, 6.4% and 10.1% respectively of the median water bill. The highest relative WTP is observed in the country with the highest number of respondents who state that they are not satisfied with the quality of their drinking water (Mexico).

Figure 2.6. **Median water bill and WTP for improved water quality**

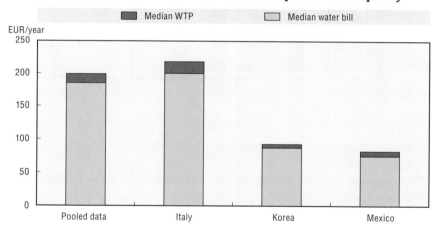

Source: OECD Project on Household Behaviour and Environmental Policy.

Income is positively related with stated WTP for improvements in the drinking water quality. The willingness-to-pay is decreasing with age. The results of other studies suggest the relationship may be nonlinear (a negative sign on age and a positive sign on age-squared). Women are found to have a lower willingness-to-pay for a better drinking water quality, and respondents with a high education level (about 9% of the whole sample) seem to be willing to pay more for water quality. The presence of young children – or other variables related to the composition of the household – was never significant in the estimations. The degree of trust the respondent has in information provided by national or local governments is found to be positively related to the WTP.

As pointed out above, exerting pressure for public sector investments in water quality services are not the only means at the disposal of households who seek to improve the quality of their drinking water. On the one hand, households can invest in purification systems. On the other hand, they can consume bottled water for their drinking needs. The proportion of respondents adopting these two strategies varies by country (see Figure 2.7).

Figure 2.7. **Percentage of households drinking tap-water by country**

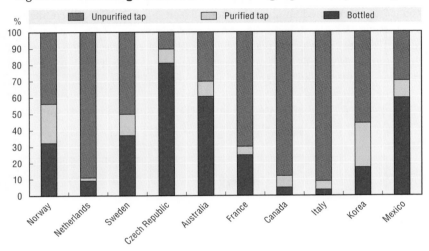

Source: OECD Project on Household Behaviour and Environmental Policy.

Countries reporting low levels of satisfaction with water (Mexico, Korea and Italy) have correspondingly high levels of bottled water consumption. Purification is less common in these three cases than in many other countries. Overall 19% of households are already equipped with, or have invested in, a water purifier in the last 10 years. Australia and Canada have the highest rates. Norway, the Netherlands and Sweden rely most heavily on "unpurified" tap-water.

Analysis of the determinants of bottled water consumption was undertaken and some of the main results are summarised in Figure 2.8. Concerns about health impacts and taste of tap-water are significant determinants of bottled water consumption. The results indicate that households that are charged for water are more likely to drink bottled water for usual drinking needs. This is consistent with economic theory (i.e. the opportunity cost of drinking bottled water is less for those who are charged for tap-water), but given the relative cost of consuming tap and bottled water the significance of the effect is surprising.

Figure 2.8. **Effects of different factors on bottled water consumption**

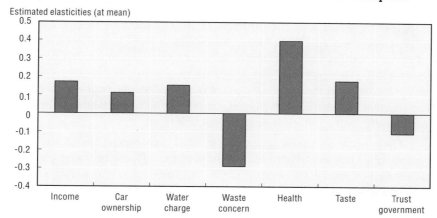

Source: OECD Project on Household Behaviour and Environmental Policy.

Other results include the finding that car ownership has a significant effect on bottled water consumption, even when the effects of other related factors (*e.g.* income, location of residence, etc.) are controlled for. Given the inconvenience associated with purchasing bottled water consumption this is not surprising. And finally, stated concern for solid waste has a negative effect on bottled water consumption. This result is robust, and very strong.

Separate analysis of the determinants of investment in purification of tap-water indicates that other factors are important. For instance, household size is positive and significant reflecting economies of scale in such investments relative to bottled water. Health is relatively more important than taste in this case. Car ownership, concern for waste and volumetric water charges have no effect on investment in purification.

5. Conclusions

First and foremost, the results show the effectiveness of charging households for the amount of water they use as a means to promote water conservation. This action alone would, on average, lower household water consumption by about 20%. While residential water consumption is found to be price inelastic, the finding that the price elasticity of demand is statistically different from zero in all ten surveyed countries indicates that an appropriate volumetric charge for water can promote water conservation. In addition, using a broader sample it has been found that volumetric charging for water increases the likelihood that households will undertake several water saving behaviours and investments.

However, respondent awareness of water consumption is relatively low. As such, the effect of metering for water consumption may be two-fold: *a*) increasing awareness of consumption; and *b*) allowing service providers to price water on a per unit basis. Awareness in and of itself seems to have an impact on investing in water-efficient appliances and undertaking water-saving behaviours. This suggests that water charges can work in tandem with water saving campaigns to reinforce desired water conservation. The positive and significant effect of eco-labels on the probability of investing in water-efficient appliances underscores this point.

The manner in which incentives and policies interact may differ across segments of the population. For instance, the effects of water charging, labelling and home ownership status on investment in water-efficient equipment are comparable in size. However, there are, of course, likely to be significant interactions between these three factors. For instance, the value of water charging and eco-labelling are likely to be very different depending upon home ownership status.

Stated concern for the environment has a significant effect on most water-saving behaviours, but it does not appear to have a significant effect on water consumption. The results of the analyses undertaken show that the decision to invest in water-efficient appliances is positively affected by respondents' environmental behaviour, as reflected in propensity to purchase "green" products in other areas. It thus seems that the respondents undertaking such investments do so in large part for environmental reasons. The marginal effect of the proxy variable for environmental behaviour far exceeds the marginal effect of income.

The results also indicated that increases in the average price of water will pose a greater burden on low-income households since they spend a much higher proportion of their income on their water bill than high income households do. This is a significant policy concern. However, it is important to keep marginal incentives intact. Full-cost water pricing, coupled with assistance to low-income households in the form of a low or zero fixed fee, or via transfer payments, will help ensure water is used efficiently and allocated equitably across residential consumers.

Concern about water quality varies by country, with concerns about health more frequently cited than taste. There are three means to address such concerns: public investment in treatment systems; private investment in purification at the level of the tap; and use of bottled water for drinking water consumption. The economic and environmental impacts of these three strategies are very different, and thus it is important to understand what motivates household preferences and choices.

It is found that WTP in improved public water treatment (as a proportion of median water bills) is relatively low, generally less than 10% of water bills. Stated WTP is affected by income, education, gender and other factors. However, it is also affected significantly by the degree of trust in government authorities. In the absence of such trust households will turn to one of the other strategies (bottled water consumption and in-house purification) to secure the desired level of quality.

However, the economic and environmental implications of which strategy is adopted are very different. Moreover, the factors which drive the adoption of each strategy are very different. In policy terms, it is interesting that concerns for solid waste have a negative effect on bottled water consumption, but not on in-house purification (as expected). This underscores the need to examine environmental issues in an integrated manner, and to design policies accordingly.

Notes

1. For instance, the European Union's Water Framework Directive states that member states will be required to ensure that the price charged to water consumers – such as for the abstraction and distribution of fresh water and the collection and treatment of waste water – reflects the true costs. Whereas this principle has a long tradition in some countries, this is currently not the case in others. However, derogations will be possible, *e.g.* in less-favoured areas or to provide basic services at an affordable price *http://ec.europa.eu/environment/water/water-framework/info/intro_en.htm*.

2. However, several empirical analyses have shown that the welfare loss of water restrictions usually exceeds that of a price increase (Woo, 1994; Roibás, García-Valiñas and Wall, 2007; Grafton and Ward, 2008).

3. A small number of unrealistic values were "cleaned" from the data. These probably reflect misunderstanding concerning the units.

4. With differentiated block tariffs, the marginal price would be a better measure, but it was not possible to obtain such data.

References

Dalhuisen, J.M., H.L.F. de Groot and P. Nijkamp (2000), "The Economics of Water: A Survey", *International Journal of Development Planning Literature*, Vol. 15(1), pp. 1-17.

Dalhuisen, J.M., R.J.G.M. Florax, H.L.F. de Groot and P. Nijkamp (2003), "Price and Income Elasticities of Residential Water Demand: A Meta-Analysis", *Land Economics*, Vol. 79(2), pp. 292-308.

Domene, E. and D. Sauri (2005), "Urbanisation and Water Consumption: Influencing Factors in the Metropolitan Region of Barcelona", *Urban Studies*, Vol. 43(9), pp. 1605-1623.

Gaudin, S. (2006), "Effect of Price Information on Residential Water Demand", *Applied Economics*, Vol. 38(4), pp. 383-393.

Hanke, S.H. and L. de Maré (1984), "Municipal Water Demands", in J. Kindler and C.S. Russell (eds.), in collaboration with B.T. Bower, I. Gouevsky, D.R. Maidment and W.R.D. Sewell, *Modeling Water Demands*, pp. 149-169, Academic Press, London.

Howe, C.W. and F.P. Linaweaver (1967), "The Impact of Price on Residential Water Demand and its Relation to System Design and Price Structure", *Water Resources Research*, Vol. 3(1), pp. 13-32.

Luzar, E.J, and K.J. Cosse, 1998. "Willingness to Pay or Intention to Pay: The Attitude-Behavior Relationship in Contingent Valuation", *Journal of Socioeconomics*, Vol. 27(3), pp. 427-444.

Lyman, R.A. (1992), "Peak and Off-Peak Residential Water Demand", *Water resources Research*, Vol. 28(9), pp. 2159-2162.

Nauges, C. and A. Thomas (2003), "Long-run Study of Residential Water Consumption", *Environmental and Resource Economics*, Vol. 26, pp. 25-43.

Nauges, C. and A. Thomas (2000), "Privately Operated Water Utilities, Municipal Price Negotiation, and Estimation of Residential Water Demand: The Case of France", *Land Economics*, Vol. 76(1), pp. 68-85.

Nieswiadomy, M.L. and D.J. Molina (1989), "Comparing Residential Water Demand Estimates under Decreasing and Increasing Block Rates using Household Data", *Land Economics*, Vol. 65(3), pp. 280-289.

Nieswiadomy, M.L. and D.J. Molina (1988), "Urban Water Demand Estimates under Increasing Block Rates", *Growth and Change*, Vol. 19(1), pp. 1-12.

OECD (2003), *Social Issues in the Provision and Pricing of Water Services*, OECD, Paris.

Renwick, M.E. and S.O. Archibald (1998), "Demand Side Management Policies for Residential Water Use: Who Bears the Conservation Burden?", *Land Economics*, Vol. 74(3), pp. 343-359.

Schleich, J. and T. Hillenbrand (2009), "Determinants of Residential Water Demand in Germany", *Ecological Economics*, Vol. 68, Issue 6, pp. 1756-1769.

Chapter 3

Residential Energy Use

> *Growing world energy demand, including from the residential sector, is putting increasing pressure on the environment and is key to addressing climate change. This chapter looks at the effect of measures available to policy makers to promote energy efficiency and the use of renewable energy. These range from economic incentives, such as energy taxation or grants for investment in solar panels, to energy efficiency labelling and communication campaigns. The main factors influencing energy-saving behaviour at home and affecting investments in energy-efficiency equipments are analysed, with particular attention paid to the role of energy pricing. The role of respondents' level of environmental concern is considered. The chapter also examines the determinants of demand for renewable energy and how much more households are willing to pay to use renewable energy.*

1. Introduction

Growing world energy demand, including from the residential sector, is putting increasing pressure on the environment and is a key challenge to address climate change. Globally, household energy consumption grew by 20% between 1990 and 2006 (IEA, 2009), accounting for almost 30% of total final consumption and 20% of end-use sectors' CO_2 emissions. Residential energy use in OECD countries is expected to increase by an average of 1.4% per year through to 2030, and this increase will be even more rapid in non-OECD countries (OECD, 2008a).

While energy demand from large appliances and space heating has been constrained by the implementation of energy efficiency policies in IEA countries, these efficiency gains have been more than offset by the rapid diffusion of new small appliances (e.g. personal computers, mobile phones and other home electronics) and the use of air conditioning. During that same period, energy consumption for space heating increased by only 5%, compared to 52% for appliances energy consumption. A number of other factors affect this trend, including income growth, changing lifestyles with smaller households, and demographic pressure.

Improving energy efficiency at home and increasing household renewable energy use is a policy goal of governments in a number of countries. The European Union objectives to reduce energy consumption by 20% by 2020 and to source 20% of its energy from renewable sources by 2020 (CEC, 2009) are an example. The OECD work on *Household Behaviour and Environmental Policy* and the 2008 Survey results provide new insight to inform the design of environmental policies targeting residential energy use on the demand side.[1]

Policies available to policy makers to promote more efficient use of energy in the residential sector, as well as the use of renewable energy, range from economic incentives (e.g. energy/carbon taxation, energy conservation grants), to information provision (e.g. energy efficiency labelling, communication campaigns) and direct regulation (e.g. energy standards for appliances).

Economic instruments are widely used to influence household energy consumption, and include energy taxes, grants and preferential loans to invest in energy efficient equipments, as well as financial incentives to promote the installation of solar panels and residential wind turbines. Funding for energy saving measures in Norway, solar incentives in France, building retrofit subsidies in the Czech Republic under the Panel Programme and a Canadian programme (*ecoENERGY Retrofit – Homes*) to provide grants to homeowners to improve the energy performance of dwellings are some examples of current measures being applied in the countries surveyed.

Energy efficiency labelling and information campaigns are another key policy measure aimed at enabling consumers to compare products and to make more informed choices. The *EU Energy Label* has been in place for over fifteen years and has proved to be successful. To promote greater public awareness on energy savings in buildings, the Energy Performance of Buildings Directive introduced an energy performance certificate which has to be produced when a house is sold or rented out.

Direct regulations targeting residential energy use are also commonly applied by governments. At the European level, minimum energy efficiency standards for new residential buildings were tightened in 2009 and the progressive phase-out of traditional light bulbs started the same year. Recent initiatives in Australia include the enforcement of new lighting standards and the phasing-out of incandescent bulbs in 2009; Korea implemented the *e-Standby Programme* with the goal of reducing the stand-by power of each electrical device below one watt by 2010, and Canada is planning as well to ban the sale of inefficient light bulbs by 2012.

In addition, governments can encourage end-use energy efficiency and promote the take up of green energy demand through well-designed energy-related public services, such as the installation of smarter metering in homes or the provision of differentiated "green" energy to residential customers. In recent years, programmes to develop smart electricity meters, allowing households to see how much energy they are using and to adjust consumption accordingly, have multiplied. Initiatives in Australia, Italy and by the Government of Ontario, in Canada, are examples, as well as the recent plan to equip every home with smart meters by the end of 2020 in the United Kingdom.

Improved understanding of the main drivers of consumers' behaviour towards residential energy use is necessary for the design of public policies promoting energy efficiency and renewable energy use. This is one objective of the OECD survey. Drawing upon observations from over 10 000 households in ten OECD countries, analysis of the survey results provides insights into key issues including:

- *Main factors influencing energy-saving behaviour at home.* Results confirm the impact of economic incentives on household behaviour. Respondents who are charged for the energy they use are more likely to undertake energy saving activities such as turning off lights. Being concerned with environmental issues also appears to have a positive effect, highlighting the significant role of information tools.

- *Main factors affecting investments in energy-efficiency equipments.* Energy metering is also found to induce more frequent investment in energy-saving equipment. Stated concern for the environment also increases the likelihood of making such investment. In addition, results show that homeowners are more likely than tenants to invest in thermal insulation and energy-efficient appliances as well as low-energy lighting.

- *Main factors motivating demand for renewable energy.* The survey results indicate that general attitude towards the environment (environmental awareness, membership of environmental organisations, etc.) strongly influences demand for renewable energy. However, the results confirm the finding from previous studies that households are not willing to pay much to use renewable energy. While there is significant variation across countries, in general respondents display a price premium of less than 5% of their bill.

This chapter presents a summary of the main survey findings concerning residential energy use. Two reports prepared for the Secretariat and presented at the OECD Conference on Household Behaviour and Environmental Policy, held in Paris 3-4 June 2009, were used as main inputs in the preparation of this chapter. The first contribution addresses residential energy efficiency and has been prepared by Milan Ščasný and Jan Urban from Charles University in Prague, the Czech Republic. The second report analyses demand for renewable energy and has been prepared by Bengt Kriström from SLU University, Sweden. The full technical reports are available at: *http://dx.doi.org/10.1787/9789264096875-en* and *www.oecd.org/environment/households/greeningbehaviour*.

The chapter is structured as follows: Section 2 examines the main determinants of energy saving behaviour at home, Section 3 looks specifically at factors influencing household investments in energy-saving equipment and the role of energy efficiency labelling, Section 4 analyses household demand for renewable energy. The last section concludes with a discussion of the main policy implications.

2. Main factors influencing energy consumption and energy-saving behaviour at home

Residential energy use typically includes space and water heating, cooking, lighting and the use of appliances and equipment. This section examines household stock of appliances and main motivations to reduce energy consumption, as well as energy saving behaviours and factors affecting them.

Differences in electric appliances ownership

As noted by Kriström (OECD, 2008b), residential energy demand is a derived demand. Energy is combined with other goods, typically a capital good (*e.g.* refrigerator, boiler), to provide a service. Total household energy demand is clearly affected by the number of appliances at home. The questionnaire collected information about whether households are equipped with certain appliances, and if so, how many appliances of a particular type they have in their primary residence. On average, the households surveyed have almost 10 electric appliances of those for which information is requested. The highest number of these appliances is found in Australia, Norway and Canada (more than 11), while Korean, Mexican and Czech households are equipped with the lowest number of the appliances (about 8). Australians come first for refrigerators and air conditioners. Norwegians have the highest number of personal computers and freezers and Swedes have the highest number of set-top boxes.

The results of empirical analysis of the data indicate that income is the most important factor influencing the number of appliances households are equipped with, in line with the literature. This is particularly the case for appliances such as washing machines, microwaves, and set-top boxes.[2] The number of appliances is also found to increase with the size of the household, but in a non-linear fashion. The average number of electric appliances owned by the household increases with age but, generally, not the number of appliances of a particular type. Home ownership also appears to have a clear positive impact on appliance ownership, while the effect of education seems to be mixed and often insignificant. Households with higher education seem to own fewer television sets and set-top boxes but more personal computers.

As to the effect of other variables, analysis of the survey responses indicates that semi-detached and detached houses are generally equipped with more appliances, and the probability of the households having an appliance increases with the size of residence. It is also worth noting that environmental concerns and pro-environmental attitudes decrease the probability of owning selected appliances such as freezers and microwaves; and have a negative influence on the total number of appliances that a household possesses.

Factors motivating a reduction in energy use

Respondents were asked how important a range of factors were in encouraging them to reduce their energy consumption. The results presented in Figure 3.1 indicate that making it less expensive to invest in energy-efficient equipment is ranked first by respondents followed by the greater availability of energy-efficient products, the easier identification of labels and the belief that environmental benefits are significant. The provision of more practical information on energy conservation measures does not appear to be as important.

A closer look at the results highlights significant country variations as indicated in Figure 3.2. Countries where respondents indicated that greater affordability of energy-saving equipment would encourage them to reduce energy consumption the most are Canada, France and Mexico. It is interesting

Figure 3.1. **Motivation to reduce energy consumption at home, OECD10**

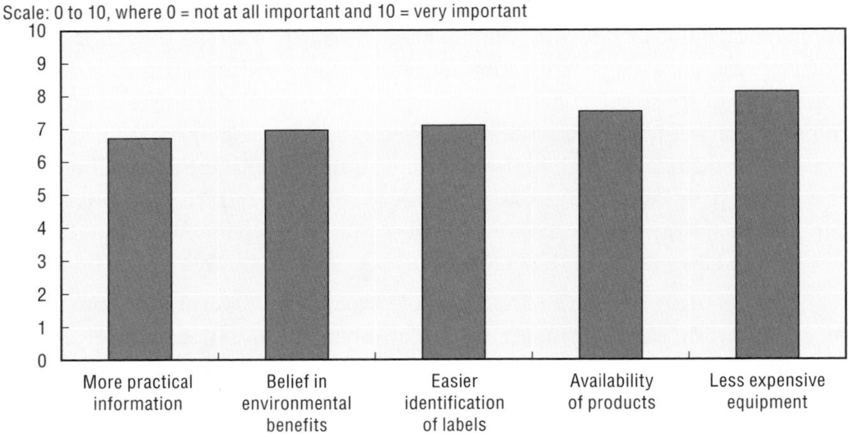

Scale: 0 to 10, where 0 = not at all important and 10 = very important

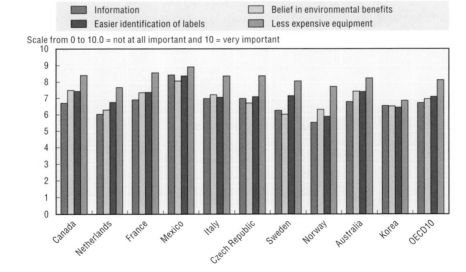

Note: The y-axis shows the average importance of each factor. Respondents were asked how important the listed factors were in encouraging them to reduce their energy consumption and these were given weights as follows: Not at all important (0), Not important (3.33), Fairly important (6.66) and Very important (10).

Source: OECD Project on Household Behaviour and Environmental Policy.

Figure 3.2. **Importance of selected factors on the motivation to reduce energy consumption, by country**

Note: The y-axis shows the average importance of each factor. Respondents were asked how important the listed factors were in encouraging them to reduce their energy consumption and these were given weights as follows: Not at all important (0), Not important (3.33), Fairly important (6.66) and Very important (10).

Source: OECD Project on Household Behaviour and Environmental Policy.

to note that the greater availability of energy-efficient appliances is ranked high in the same countries. Importance attached to the belief that environmental benefits of energy savings are significant appears to be the greatest for Australia, Canada and Mexico. Results also suggest that the provision of more practical information on energy conservation measures is generally not ranked high, with the exception of Mexico.

Main determinants of energy saving behaviour

Data were collected on households' energy saving behaviour. Five types of energy-saving activities are distinguished: switching off lights when leaving a room, cutting down on air conditioning or heating to limit energy consumption, energy-efficient use of washing machines or dishwashers, turning off appliances when not in use, and turning off the stand-by mode of appliances/electronic devices.

Energy saving patterns

General patterns in energy saving behaviour in the 10 countries surveyed are presented in Figure 3.3. The survey responses show that turning off the light when leaving a room is the most common energy-saving activity, followed by economical use of dishwashers and washing machines, and

Figure 3.3. **Differences in energy saving behaviours, OECD10**

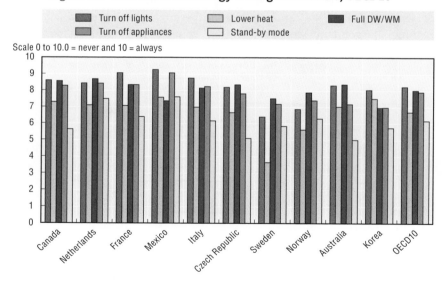

Note: The y-axis shows the reported frequency of each practice. Responses were given weights as follows: Never (0), Occasionally (3.33), Often (6.66) and Always (10).

Source: OECD Project on Household Behaviour and Environmental Policy.

turning off the appliances when not in use. On the other hand, cutting down on heating and air conditioning to limit energy consumption is not performed very often and turning off the stand-by mode of appliances and electronic devices is the most rarely reported.

However, great variations across countries exist. The Dutch are the most likely to turn off their electronic appliances and devices while Australia, the Czech Republic and Korea have the highest percentage of respondents reporting that they never or occasionally switch off stand-by mode (approximately 50%). Norwegians and Swedes reported turning off lights when leaving a room less often than respondents from other countries. Results also suggest that Koreans are the least likely to wait for full loads before using washing machines or dishwashers.

The role of metering

The results confirm the impact of economic incentives on household behaviour. Econometric analysis of the determinants of energy saving behaviour points to the significant and positive effect of energy metering. As shown in Figure 3.4, respondents who are charged for the energy they use reported significantly more frequent energy saving behaviour, with the exception of turning off appliances when not in use and turning off the stand-by mode.

In OECD countries, some households pay a variable electricity price according to the time of use. They generally pay a lower price during off-peak period (e.g. night time) and a higher price during peak period (e.g. early evening). Respondents were asked if they were charged according to the time

Figure 3.4. **Energy saving behaviour: Influence of being metered**

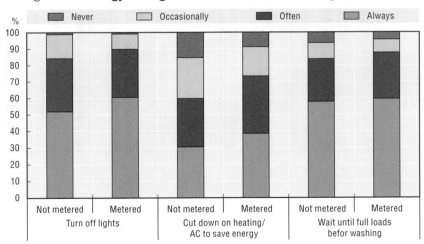

Source: OECD Project on Household Behaviour and Environmental Policy.

of use. The proportion of households who reported paying a lower price during off-peak period and a higher price during peak period varies widely by country, from 11% in Norway to 75% in Mexico.

Households who are charged a variable electricity rate were in general more likely to undertake energy saving behaviour with the exception of running only full washing machines and dishwasher loads, where the responses were similar. Variable charging has less of an impact on this particular energy-saving behaviour since households may prefer to take advantage of lower rates during off-peak hours and use their washing machines even if not fully loaded. This suggests that time-of-day pricing may lead to higher consumption as households substitute some usage from one part of the day to another (see Figure 3.5).

Figure 3.5. **Energy saving behaviour: Influence of variable electricity charge according to time of use**

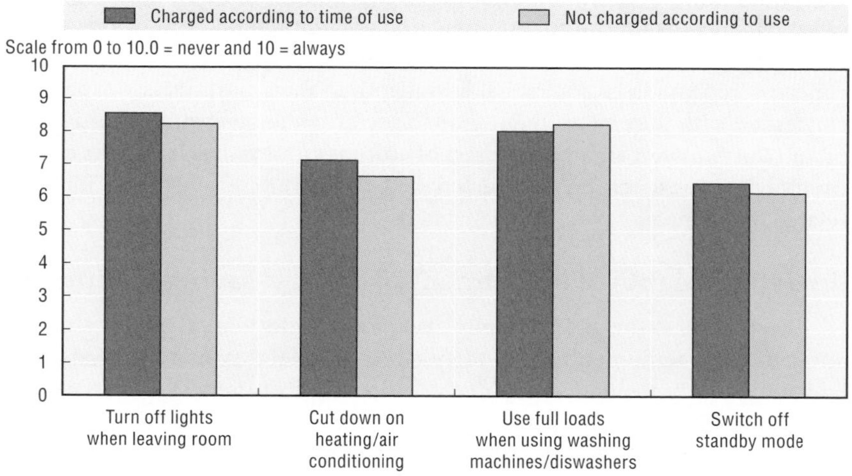

Note: The y-axis shows the average frequency of behaviour. Respondents were asked how often they performed the listed behaviours: Never, Occasionally, Often and Always. The responses were given a weight of 0.00, 3.33, 6.66, 10.00 respectively.
Source: OECD Project on Household Behaviour and Environmental Policy.

The role of environmental concerns and other factors

Econometric analysis indicates that men generally tend to perform energy saving activities less often than women, as well as wealthier people. This negative and significant effect of income on all energy-conserving behaviours examined contrasts with previous studies where income is frequently found to have a mixed effect. High-income households might be less willing to trade their comfort and time for energy savings and/or they tend to invest in energy efficient equipment to achieve energy savings as discussed in the next section.

Attainment of a higher education level is found to have only a weak and negative effect in the case of switching off the light, a pattern that has also been identified in the literature. Previous studies, however, generally show mixed results. On the one hand, higher education appears to lead to a better understanding of energy conservation (Black *et al.*, 1985; Laquatra and Chi, 1988) and tends to be associated with environmental consciousness and thus with higher frequency of energy-conservation practices (Hogan, 1976). On the other hand, education is also sometimes associated with a negative effect on energy conservation behaviour (Hirst and Goeltz, 1984; Peters, 1990; Curtis *et al.*, 1984).

Other variables of importance include the area of residence and those living in urban areas appear to be less likely to perform energy-saving activities. Besides, we can note that respondents who reported taking into account environmental labels when purchasing a good were also more likely to undertake energy-saving activities.

Last but not least, the analysis points to the positive and relatively strong effect of concerns for the environment and environmental attitudes on energy-saving behaviours, which is another policy-relevant finding. The effect of concerns appears to be somewhat stronger than that of attitudes. Respondents concerned with the environment tend to perform energy-saving activities more often. The relatively significant effect of attitudes and values is new, as much of the previous research has suggested that these variables are only indirectly related to actual energy-saving behaviour.

3. Main determinants of investment in energy-saving equipments

Responses to the questionnaire also provide information on investment in energy-saving equipment. Respondents were asked if they had installed in their current primary residence any of the following five items over the past ten years: energy-efficiency-rated appliances (*e.g.* top rated washing machines, refrigerators), low-energy light bulbs (compact fluorescent), thermal insulation (*e.g.* walls/roof insulation, double-glazing), efficient heating boiler (*e.g.* condensing boiler), or renewable energy (*e.g.* solar panels, wind turbines).

Investment in energy-saving equipments: general pattern

The percentage of respondents who reported having installed low-energy light bulbs in their current primary residence over the past ten years is quite similar in all ten countries (around 70% for the whole sample), except for Korea (28%). Investment in low-energy light bulbs and in energy-efficient appliances is followed by insulation and the installation of efficient heating boilers. As expected, the percentage of respondents reporting having installed renewable energy is very low (around 5% for the whole sample). Norway is an exception with more than 15% (see Figure 3.6).

Figure 3.6. **Investment in energy-saving equipment**

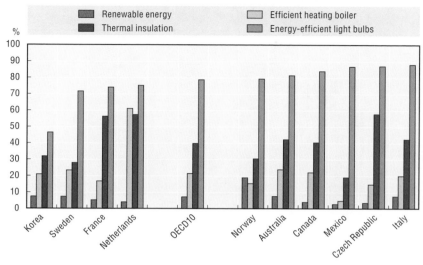

Note: The proportion of households installing energy efficient equipment in the last 10 years in their primary residence, by country. The results are calculated excluding those households that were already equipped and those who reported that it was not possible to install such equipment.

Source: OECD Project on Household Behaviour and Environmental Policy.

The importance of being metered

The results of econometric analysis show that metering matters. The role of energy charges in encouraging energy-saving investments is clearly evident in the survey responses. As in the case of energy-saving behaviours, respondents who are charged for the energy they use reported significantly greater probability of having invested in energy-saving equipment (see Figure 3.7).

The role of labelling

There is a high level of recognition of energy-efficient appliance labels in the majority of the ten surveyed countries (Figure 3.8). Nearly 80% of survey respondents recognise energy-efficient appliance labels. Label recognition was highest in Australia, Korea, Canada and the Netherlands at 98%, 96%, 91% and 90% respectively, and lowest in Sweden (41%) and Norway (66%). The Czech Republic has the highest reported installation rate of energy-efficiency-rated appliances at 77% despite their relatively low levels of label recognition and use compared with other countries. The gap between the level of recognition of appliance energy-efficiency labels and reported installation is high in Korea, Canada, Australia and the Netherlands, and the lowest in Sweden and Norway.

Figure 3.7. **Investing in energy-saving equipment: Impact of metering**

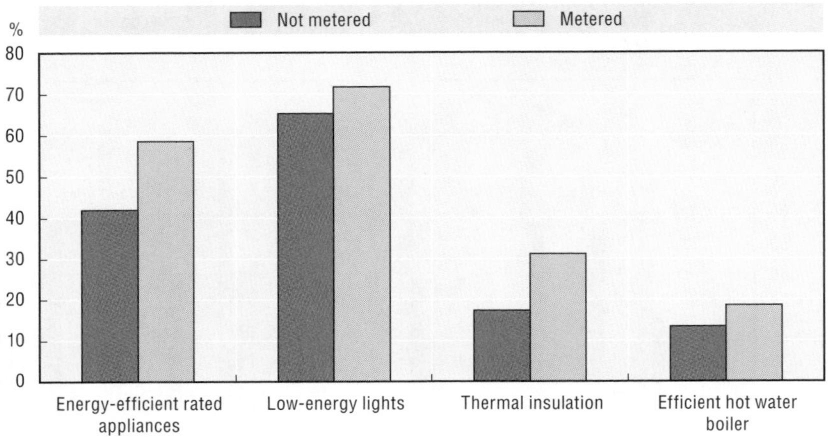

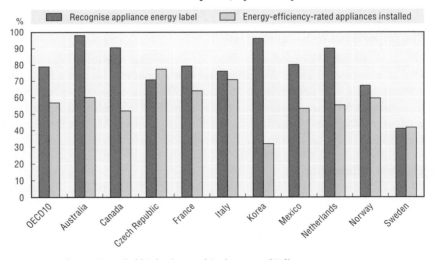

Source: OECD Project on Household Behaviour and Environmental Policy.

Figure 3.8. **Proportion of households who recognise appliance energy labels and who have installed energy efficiency rated appliances in the last 10 years, by country**

Source: OECD Project on Household Behaviour and Environmental Policy.

Simpler labelling of energy efficiency was ranked on average as the third most important factor of energy savings but it appears to be less important in Korea, the Netherlands and Norway. Moreover, Czechs, Dutch, Mexicans and Swedes ranked simpler identification of labels as being more important than environmental benefits.

Households were also asked if they took energy costs into account when purchasing or renting their home (Figure 3.9). Overall, 30% of respondents took energy costs into account and this varied from 49% in the Czech Republic to 19% in Australia and the Netherlands. France and Canada have introduced labels that indicate the relative energy efficiency of houses, these have similar levels of recognition in both countries (60%).

Figure 3.9. **Proportion of households taking into account energy costs when purchasing or renting their current primary residence**

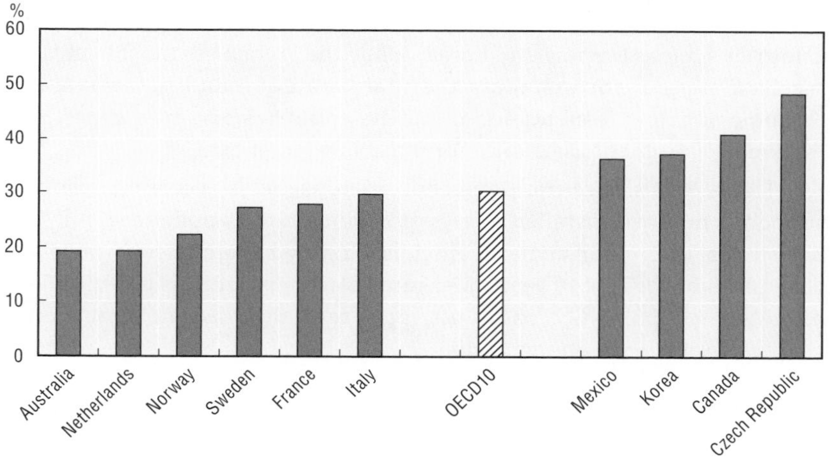

Source: OECD Project on Household Behaviour and Environmental Policy.

Respondents were asked to rank different sources of information on environmental issues in terms of their trustworthiness. It is interesting to note that people who trust the government are more likely to use energy efficiency labels, 62% compared to 56%. Trust in information provision is likely to be particularly important in the face of cases of product information compliance breaches, such as those recently reported in the United Kingdom for household appliances not meeting the energy performance levels displayed on energy-efficiency labels.

An econometric analysis of the factors affecting the recognition of energy efficiency labels for appliances and for houses when they are available shows that men are more likely to recognise energy-efficiency labels, while women know the general ecological labels better. Older people are found to have generally less knowledge of the labels displayed. Furthermore education increases the probability of recognising general environmental labels. Income has a positive and significant effect only in the case of the efficient appliance label and general ecological labels. Results also suggest that people who live in larger cities know the ecological labels better, but they have less knowledge of the energy-efficiency labels for houses than people living in rural areas. The label for energy saving houses is known better to those who own their dwellings. In all cases, pro-environmental attitudes and concerns increase the probability of label recognition.

The use of government support schemes

The proportion of households receiving government support when installing energy-efficient items varies depending on the country and the item, rates being higher for renewable energy and in general lower in countries such as Norway and Korea. While the French are most likely to have received support for installing thermal insulation and renewable energy technologies, few respondents in all the countries surveyed report having received government assistance for those investments.

Figure 3.10 shows the proportion of households receiving government support who have installed energy efficiency rated appliances, low energy light bulbs, thermal insulation, efficient heating boilers or renewable energy generators in the last 10 years. Measures considered in this question include monetary support such as grants, preferential loans and non-monetary support, for instance energy audits.

Figure 3.10. **Proportion of households benefiting from government support when installing energy efficient equipment, by country**

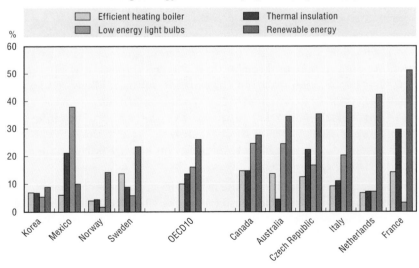

Source: OECD Project on Household Behaviour and Environmental Policy.

The proportion of households receiving government support when installing energy-efficient items varies depending on the country and the item, rates being highest for renewable energy and lowest for efficient heating boilers. Thirteen per cent of those installing efficiency rated appliances received some type of government support. A significant proportion of those installing low energy light bulbs have received government support, 16% on average with the top three countries being Australia (24%), Canada (25%) and Mexico. The rate of government support for thermal insulation is 14% for the survey countries with the top two being France (30%) and the Czech Republic (22%). Support rates for installing energy-efficient heating boilers vary from 4% in Norway to 15% in Canada, with 10% overall. Renewable energy, for example solar panel and wind turbines, has the highest proportion attracting government support with 51% in France, 42% in the Netherlands, 38% in Italy, 35% in the Czech Republic and 34% in Australia.

The results show that nearly one quarter of households installing one of the listed energy efficient items received some type of government support. Government support rates are lowest in Norway, Sweden and Korea at 5%, 10% and 13% respectively. The rate of households receiving government support to install thermal insulation and renewable energy does not differ notably by income level, with the exception of those installing renewable energy, where a greater proportion of high income households (31%) received government support when compared to medium (24%) and low income households (25%) (see Figure 3.11).

Figure 3.11. **Proportion of households benefiting from some government support who have installed thermal insulation or renewable energy in the past 10 years by income bracket**

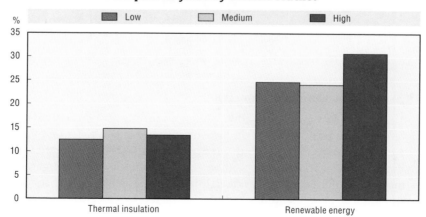

Source: OECD Project on Household Behaviour and Environmental Policy.

Differences across households

The results of an econometric analysis of the decision to install different types of energy-efficient equipment clearly indicate that the status on the property market matters. Home ownership has a positive effect on the probability of installing energy-saving equipment or renewable energy technologies (Figure 3.12). This pattern can be explained by the importance of "split incentives", with renters being less likely to recover the sunk costs associated with such investments. However, it is striking that this also seems to be the case with the installation of low energy bulbs, which are relatively low-cost and transferable. These results underline the usefulness of targeting measures according to home ownership status as in the United Kingdom where the Landlord's Energy Saving Allowance (LESA) has been introduced.[3]

Figure 3.12. **Percentage of households having installed energy-saving equipment according to home ownership status**

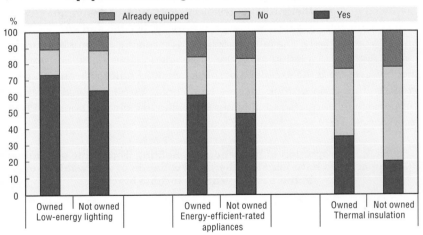

Source: OECD Project on Household Behaviour and Environmental Policy.

The role of environmental concerns

Econometric analysis shows that environmental concerns have a significant and positive effect on investment in energy-efficient equipment. The effect of environmental attitudes is less marked. Results indicate that environmental awareness and membership in an environmental organisation is highly correlated with the decision to invest. Households for whom environmental benefits are ranked high as factors which encourage them to reduce energy consumption are more likely to have installed energy-efficiency-rated appliances in their primary residence in the last 10 years than other households (see Figure 3.13).

Willingness-to-pay more to use renewable energy

Respondents were also asked what was the maximum percentage increase on their annual bill they were willing to pay to use only renewable energy, assuming that their energy consumption remained constant.

Survey responses indicate that respondents are not willing to pay much. Figure 3.15 shows that almost half of all respondents are not willing to pay anything to use only green energy and that respondents are not ready to pay more than 5% above their current electricity bill, on average, to use only green energy.[5] These findings are in line with previous studies. However, there is significant variation across countries with Dutch respondents showing the lowest mean willingness-to-pay a price premium to use only green energy, followed by France and Korea. One could argue that the market in the Netherlands is saturated because a large amount of green energy is already provided in the energy mix, so that WTP at the margin is not very high.

Figure 3.15. **Willingness-to-pay for renewable energy**

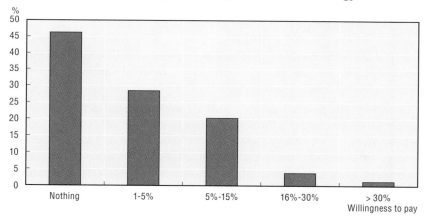

Source: OECD Project on Household Behaviour and Environmental Policy.

The econometric analysis of the determinants of willingness-to-pay (WTP) to use renewable energy undertaken proceeds in two steps: those who are "enter the market" (willing to pay something) are first examined and a particular analysis is then undertaken on the decision to "enter the market" or not.

The model predicts a lower WTP for women, which, to some extent, contradicts earlier findings in the literature on the valuation of environmental quality (see Farreras *et al.*, 2005 for a review). Next, people who find environmental issues relatively unimportant display a lower WTP. Finally, being a member of an environmental organisation has a significantly positive effect on the level of WTP to use "green" electricity. These results stressing the importance of attitudinal factors are in line with previous studies (Rowlands *et al.*, 2003; Roe *et al.*, 2001).

Surprisingly, household income seems to play little, if any role when the WTP is positive. However, the link between income and the decision to "enter the market" is positive in the model used. In the econometric analysis, age is also found to be a significant predictor for the decision to pay something, but not for the level of WTP. Thus, older people are less likely to pay a premium to use renewable electricity. In addition, the probability of entering the market increases with education. Finally, attitudes towards the environment and activities/membership of environmental organisations have a positive impact on the decision to pay more to use renewable energy.

5. Conclusions and policy implications

Several policy implications emerge from this new work on the determinants of household residential energy use. First of all, the survey clearly confirms the significant role played by incentive-based policy instruments to reduce energy demand from households. Electricity metering (and charging) encourages energy-saving behaviour. Results show that respondents paying charges are more likely to save energy, whether by adopting energy-saving behaviour like turning off lights, or making investments in efficiency-rated appliances and thermal insulation.

In addition, people's attitude towards the environment appears to clearly influence energy demand. The survey shows that environmental awareness has a positive effect on energy-saving behaviour at home and on investments in energy-efficient equipment. Being concerned with the environment and membership in environmental organisations, is associated with increased demand for renewable energy. This evidence implies that "softer" instruments, based on the provision of information to consumers and education, can have a substantial complementary role to raise people's environmental awareness.

Furthermore, the survey highlights the importance of targeting measures on certain population groups in some cases, since not all households face the same incentives to make environmentally-friendly energy investments. Indeed, the findings reveal that homeowners are more likely than tenants to invest in energy-saving equipment such as thermal insulation or efficient heating boilers, as well as renewable energy technologies. Thus, policies where landlords are given incentives to "green" their rental properties and tenants are given the right to recover their costs for such investments from landlords could be usefully implemented. However, targeting policies can entail significant costs that need to be taken into account.

Finally, the results also suggest that the substantial support given to renewable energy in many countries contrasts with the fairly weak voluntary demand for "green" electricity reported in this survey. While there is significant variation across countries, the survey shows that respondents are not willing to pay too much more to use green energy. This is in line with previous studies. Indeed, relatively few households are prepared to pay more than 5% above their current electricity bill to use green energy, and almost half of them are not willing to pay anything. This finding implies that the increased use of green energy at home in the future is likely to be only weakly demand-driven, and thus might heavily rely upon policy measures targeting the supply side.

Notes

1. The impact of policies focussing on the supply side, such as government incentives to develop renewable energy technologies, is outside the scope of this study.

2. A set-top box is a small computing device that interfaces a television (TV) set or computer to a cable TV network, cable modem network and, perhaps, telephone network.

3. This scheme seeks to encourage energy efficiency in the residential rented sector by allowing landlords to deduct from their taxable profits the costs of acquiring and installing certain energy-saving equipment in properties they let.

4. Respondents who state that they were not given this option have been removed from the sample.

5. Calculations show that the conditional "mean" is in the interval 7.4%-9.1%. Factoring in the 46.2% zero WTP, we obtain the bounds 4%-4.9%.

References

Black, S., P. Stern and J. Elworth (1985), "Personal and Contextual Influences on Household Energy Adaptations", *Journal of Applied Psychology*, Vol. 70(1), pp. 3-21.

CEC (2009), "Directive 2009/28/EC of the European Parliament and of the Council of 23 April 2009 on the Promotion of the Use of Energy from Renewable Sources and Amending and Subsequently Repealing Directives 2001/77/EC and 2003/30/EC", in *Official Journal of the European Communities*, 5 June 2009, L 140/16.

Curtis, F., P. Simpson-Housley and S. Drever (1984), "Household Energy Conservation", *Energy Policy*, Vol. 12(4), pp. 452-456.

Farreras, V., P. Riera and J. Mogas (2005), "Does Gender Matter in Valuation Studies? Evidence from Three Forestry Applications", *Forestry*, Vol. 78(3).

Hirst, E. and R. Goeltz (1984), *Comparison of Actual and Predicted Energy Savings in Minnesota Gas-heated Single-family Homes*, Oak Ridge National Laboratory, Oak Ridge, TN.

Hogan, M.J. (1976), *Energy-Conservation: Family Values, Household, Practices, and Contextual Variables* (Doctoral dissertation), Michigan State University.

International Energy Agency (2009), *World Energy Outlook 2009*, IEA, Paris.

Laquatra, J. and P. Chi (1988), "Why Home Owners Respond to Residential Energy Conservation", in Sixth Annual International Energy Efficient Building Conference and Exposition, Portland, pp. J.2-J.19, OR: Energy Efficiency Building Association, Portland.

OECD (2008a), *Environmental Outlook to 2030*, OECD, Paris.

OECD (2008b), *Household Behaviour and the Environment: Reviewing the Evidence*, OECD, Paris.

Peters, J. (1990), "Integrating Psychological and Economic Perspective of Thermostat Setting Behaviour", *American Council for an Energy Efficient Economy*, Washington DC.

Roe, B., M.F. Teisl, A.Levy and M. Russell (2001), "US Consumers' Willingness to Pay for Green Electricity", *Energy Policy*, Vol. 29, No. 11, pp. 917-925.

Rowlands, I.H., D. Scott and P. Parker (2003), "Consumers and Green Electricity: Profiling Potential Purchasers", *Business Strategy and the Environment*, Vol. 12, Issue 1, pp. 36-48.

Chapter 4

Waste Generation, Recycling and Prevention

Addressing the issue of municipal solid waste is a challenge and households are directly responsible for the generation of a large proportion of municipal waste. This chapter summarises results which improve our understanding of household behaviour with respect to waste, assisting policy makers in the design of efficient policies that induce people to minimise waste through waste recycling and prevention. This chapter addresses key policy issues such as the impact of waste charges on waste generation and recycling rates and waste prevention efforts. The question of whether the presence and characteristics of recycling programmes (e.g. door-to-door, drop-off, frequency of pick up) significantly affect the generation of mixed waste for disposal and waste recycling is examined. The role of general attitudes towards the environment in influencing household behaviour is considered as well.

1. Introduction

Environmental pressures from households are significant and their impacts are likely to intensify over the next two decades (OECD, 2008a). Addressing the issue of municipal solid waste is a challenge, and many countries are seeking to reduce waste generation and manage waste more effectively and efficiently. Households are directly responsible for a large proportion of municipal waste. For instance, in 2005, households produced over 75% of municipal waste in Korea, Germany, the United Kingdom, Mexico, Belgium, the Netherlands, the Slovak Republic, Luxembourg, Denmark, and Spain (OECD, 2008c).[1]

The growing concern for municipal waste generation and disposal stems from three important phenomena:

i)   Increased awareness of the environmental effects of waste generation through its contribution to climate change, surface and ground water contamination, and air contamination.

ii) Reluctance by governments (and resistance by communities) to the establishment of new landfills and incineration facilities.

iii) Drastic growth in municipal waste (household waste, in particular) over the last decades as a result of higher incomes, more intensive use of packaging materials and disposable goods, and increased purchases of durable material goods.

Within the OECD region, municipal waste generation increased by about 58% from 1980 to 2000 and 4.6% between 2000 and 2005; under the assumption of no new policies, total municipal waste is projected to increase by 38% from 2005 to 2030 and per capita municipal waste by 25% (from 557 kg to 694 kg) over the same period (OECD, 2008a).

In terms of waste management practices, there have been considerable changes in the relative amounts of waste being landfilled, incinerated or otherwise treated, and recycled or composted. In the mid-1990s, approximately 64% of municipal waste was destined for landfills, 18% for incineration, and 18% for recycling (OECD, 2001). However, by 2005, 49% was landfilled, 21% incinerated or otherwise treated, and 30% recycled or composted (OECD, 2007). Although the amount of waste within OECD countries being landfilled decreased not only in relative terms but also in absolute terms (from 346 to

320 million tonnes per year) during the 10-year period, seven countries still sent more than 80% of their municipal waste to landfills and two almost all of their waste in 2005 (OECD, 2008a).

In response to the increasing environmental pressures of municipal waste, many countries are exploring ways of reducing and disposing of it more effectively. Municipal governments, which tend to be responsible for carrying out waste management and recycling services and for developing waste management programs, have grown particularly interested in experimenting with unit pricing systems and improving recycling services. In the United States, for example, the number of jurisdictions with some sort of pay-as-you-throw or unit pricing programme increased from about 1 000 in 1993 to almost 7 100 in 2006 or about 25% of all US communities (Skumatz and Freeman, 2007). In Canada, the share of households with access to at least one type of recycling programme increased from about 70% in 1994 to 93% in 2006, with paper recycling experiencing the lowest increase from 70% to 88% and plastic recycling the largest increase from 63% to 87% (Statistics Canada, 2008).

To assist policy makers in the design of efficient policies that effectively induce households to minimise waste through waste prevention and/or recycling, a better understanding of household behaviour is however necessary. The OECD survey collected data on household waste generation, recycling and prevention, as well as the local policy context. Some of the key policy questions addressed include:

i)   Whether or not user fees for waste disposal have significant effects on waste generation, recycling rates and waste prevention efforts.

ii)   Whether or not the presence of a recycling programme significantly affects generation of mixed waste for disposal and waste recycling.

iii) The extent to which household waste recycling decisions depend on the attributes of recycling programs (e.g. door-to-door, drop-off, frequency of pick up) and whether there is significant variation across materials.

iv)   How general attitudes towards the environment (e.g. environmental awareness, membership of environmental organisations) influence waste generation and recycling levels.

v)   Whether the presence of economic incentives and/or other forms of governmental intervention (e.g. mandatory recycling) erodes or enhances the relevance of intrinsic motivation.[2]

This chapter is based on reports prepared for the OECD by Kwang-Yim Kim (Korean Environment Institute) on waste generation and by Ida Ferrara (York University, Canada) on waste recycling and waste prevention. The full technical reports are available at: http://dx.doi.org/10.1787/9789264096875-en and www.oecd.org/environment/households/greeningbehaviour.

The main conclusions of the work undertaken can be summarised as follows:

- Unit pricing by volume affects waste generation rates and the rate of recycling. However, it has a limited impact on the decision to recycle or not.

- The provision of recycling services has an even greater impact on recycling. It must be borne in mind, however, that it would be not have any impact (or even a positive impact) on waste generation.

- There is a significant difference in the effect of collection of recyclables door-to-door, and drop-off systems. The costs associated with the former system are likely to be much greater, and this must be taken into account.

- Waste charges have little apparent effect on waste prevention, although this is an area which is difficult to address empirically.

- Stated concern for environmental matters and social motivations have an important influence on waste management decisions. These should be taken into account in policy design, *e.g.* through the use of "soft" instruments.

The remainder of this chapter is structured as follows: Section 2 reviews the evidence on mixed waste generation; Section 3 addresses recycling behaviour distinguishing between four materials (plastics, paper, metals and glass); Section 4 reviews the relatively limited evidence on waste prevention; and, Section 5 concludes with a summary of the main policy-relevant results.

2. Waste generation

In the questionnaire respondents were requested to indicate how many bags of waste they put out for disposal each week. Given differences in standard bag size by country, a visual image was provided to assist respondents.

Despite the image, there is likely to be some bias across countries depending upon bag size commonly used. Figure 4.1 presents the frequency of responses for the full sample. Households with one person produce on average two bags of mixed waste per week, compared to 2½ bags for two person households and 3.2 bags for three person households. The amount of mixed waste per person decreases notably as household size rises, from 2 bags for a one person household to 1¼ bags per person for a 2 person household and to just over one bag per person for a 3 person household.

Casual inspection of the data indicates that waste policies may have an effect on waste generation rates. Figure 4.2 shows the average number of bags put out for disposal by those households according to whether they pay for disposal by volume and/or have a curbside recycling scheme available. The effect of recycling schemes and unit-based waste fees on waste generation is evident, with some evidence of complementarity (at least at the descriptive level).

Figure 4.1. **Household generation of mixed waste for disposal**

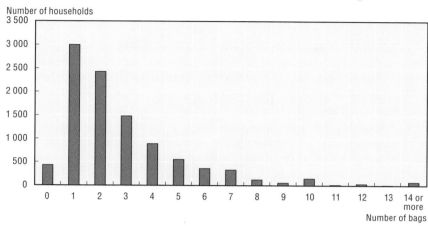

Source: OECD Project on Household Behaviour and Environmental Policy.

Figure 4.2. **Relationship between waste generation and waste policies**

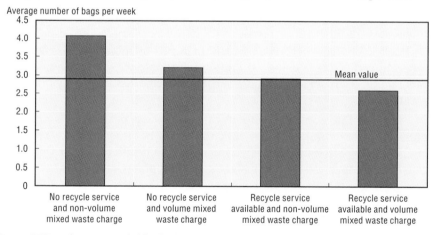

Source: OECD Project on Household Behaviour and Environmental Policy.

However, simple correlation between policy variables and waste generation rates may be misleading, and so as in the other areas more formal empirical analysis was undertaken. A number of socio-demographic variables have an impact on waste generation. For instance, holding other factors constant, respondents between 18 years and 24 years of age generate 9.38% more than the reference age group (those over 55 years of age). As the number of adults, children under 5 and children between 5-18 years old increases by 1 individual, mixed waste generation increases by 14.21%, 16.64% and 11.37%, respectively. Household waste generation increases by 0.84% as yearly income increases by EUR 10 000, although there is considerable variation in the effect across countries.

Respondents' attitudes toward the relative importance of environmental concerns (relative to five other economic and social concerns) have a negative impact on waste generation – i.e. waste generation decreases as the ranking of environmental concerns increases. The magnitude of the effect is 1.93% as the ranking of environmental problems increases by one unit (out of six). Another index measuring environmental attitudes in terms of the respondents' degree of agreement or disagreement with five statements has a negative impact, and thus waste generation decreases by 5.64% as the index (scaled between –2 and 2) increases by one unit.

The two primary policy variables that are likely to have an impact on the generation of mixed waste bags are the presence of a waste charge and the frequency of collection services. According to the estimated results, fees based on the volume of mixed waste generated have a statistically significant and negative impact on waste generation. The implementation of a volume based fee causes households to reduce waste generation by 7.11%. While the effect of weight-based fees is not statistically significant, only 2% of respondents are subject to such a fee.

Collection frequency has an important impact on mixed waste generation. When mixed waste is collected more often than once a week, households generate 19.97% more waste than when it is collected less frequently than once a week.

Much of the motivation for reducing solid waste generation is financial, rather than environmental. However, while non-hazardous solid waste does not generally pose significant environmental and health concerns, this is not true of hazardous wastes. For instance, the inappropriate disposal of wastes bearing heavy metals can have very significant impacts. Figure 4.3 presents data on whether households disposed of batteries and medicines properly (i.e. not disposed of as part of household mixed waste).

As expected, respondents' stated concern for environmental matters is highly correlated with the propensity to dispose of household hazardous waste properly (see Figure 4.4). Indeed, empirical analysis confirms that this is the most important determinant, alongside age (with older respondents more likely to dispose of both waste streams properly), and country fixed effects for both types of waste.

Figure 4.3. **Percentage of households reporting that they disposed of hazardous household waste properly**

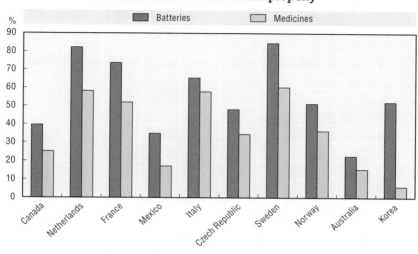

Source: OECD Project on Household Behaviour and Environmental Policy.

Figure 4.4. **Relationship between environmental attitude and percentage of households reporting that they disposed of hazardous household waste properly**

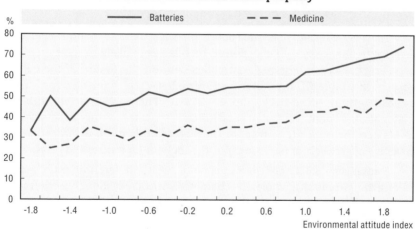

Source: OECD Project on Household Behaviour and Environmental Policy.

3. Waste recycling

Respondents were also requested to indicate how many of five different materials (glass bottles and containers; plastic bottles and containers, aluminium, tin and steel cans; paper and cardboard; and food or garden waste) they recycled. Figure 4.5 presents data on the average number of materials for which households recycled at least some of the waste generated.[3] While there is significant variation across countries it is important to note that these differences reflect differences in both household practice and service availability.

Figure 4.5. **Average number of materials recycled per household**

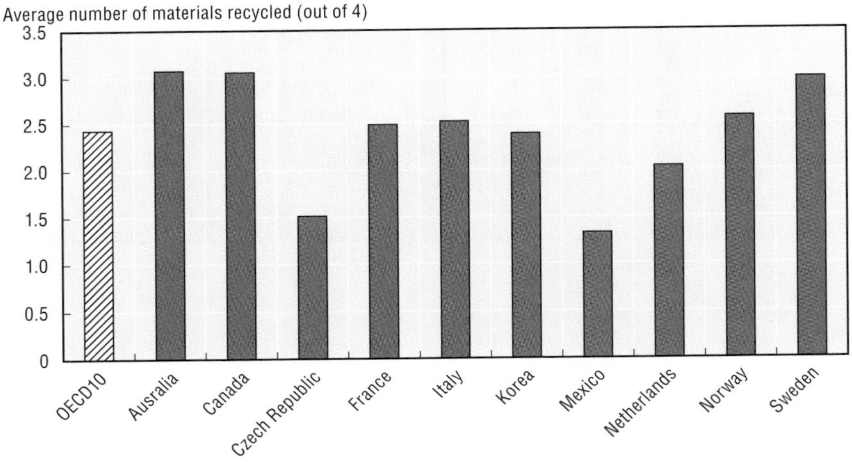

Average number of materials recycled (out of 4)

Source: OECD Project on Household Behaviour and Environmental Policy.

However, the data presented above appear to indicate that the availability of a convenient service for collection of recyclables is likely to have an effect on recycling behaviour. Figure 4.6 provides data on the nature of the collection service available (if any), distinguishing between: door-to-door; drop-off; deposit-refund; bring-back; and no service. There is variation both across materials and countries. Canada and Korea have wide coverage of services, while in Mexico the opposite is true. In the Netherlands there is almost complete coverage of services for paper and plastics, but not for metals and glass.

Simple availability of a service is not a sufficient determinant of recycling. Taking the sample as a whole, the characteristics of recycling collection services appear to have an impact on the likelihood of recycling. Figure 4.7 shows the percentage of households reporting that they recycled the material in question relative to whether or not the collection service was "door-to-door" or "drop-off". Somewhat surprisingly the difference is greatest for metal cans, which are neither the bulkiest nor the heaviest waste type.

However, there could be a number of related factors at play, and as a consequence multivariate empirical analysis was undertaken in which demographic, economic and policy factors were included as determinants.

Figure 4.6. **Recycling service availability and rates**

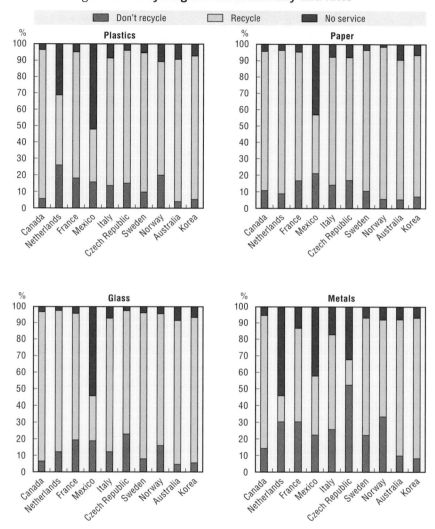

Source: OECD Project on Household Behaviour and Environmental Policy.

Moreover, the decisions of recycling different materials are likely to be correlated, and as such the equations for the different materials were estimated simultaneously in a single model.

Focussing on the policy-relevant results, there is evidence supporting the importance of attitudinal characteristics in recycling decisions. For instance, the index summarising individuals' environmental attitudes based on the

Figure 4.7. **Recycling rates and convenience of service**

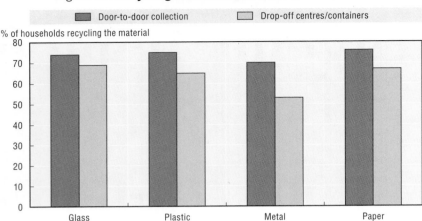

Source: OECD Project on Household Behaviour and Environmental Policy.

extent of agreement or disagreement with five statements about the environment, increases recycling for glass, plastic, and aluminium.

Expressed in terms of marginal effects, a unit increase in the index, holding the other explanatory variables at their mean values, increases the probability of recycling participation by approximately 4% for aluminium and 1% for glass and plastic. However, the results using other measures of environmental norms or concern are less robust.

Volume-based charges do not have a significant impact on the decision to recycle or not. However, amongst households who do recycle at least some of their waste volume-based charges do have a significant and positive effect on recycling intensity for every material but plastic. Conversely, the presence of a unit pricing based on weight or frequency does not have a strong effect on recycling decisions. However, it must be borne in mind that few households face a weight-based fee, and there is no *a priori* reason to expect a frequency-based fee system to increase recycling. In general, therefore, the results do suggest that economic instruments (*i.e.* user fees for waste disposal) can promote recycling, but the evidence is not as convincing as that found in other studies (*e.g.* Dijkgraaf and Gradus, 2004; Ferrara and Missios, 2005).

Recycling programmes appear to have a clear impact. The availability of curbside recycling has its greatest impact on the probability of recycling aluminium, which increases by approximately 43% compared to 21% for plastic, 16% for paper, and 11% for glass. Under a drop off system, the largest impact on recycling participation is also detected for aluminium with a 34% increase. The availability of curbside recycling results in a 15% increase on plastics, while for both glass and paper the figure is 11%.

It is important to determine whether or not the two measures (unit pricing and collection services) are complements. When unit pricing is assessed in conjunction with collection services for recyclables, the evidence does not suggest that the presence of collection programs for recyclables is likely to increase the effectiveness of unit pricing.[4] Hence, collection services for recyclables and unit pricing may be substitute policies. This result is different from that reported elsewhere that unit pricing is more effective if combined with curbside recycling and *vice versa* (Callan and Thomas, 1997).

There is also evidence that respondents view recycling as a community or public service, above and beyond the effect (if any) on environmental conditions. This is an important issue because it can have implications on policy design. Fortunately it has been possible to assess the importance of this effect through the analysis of responses to the following question:

If the (waste collection and recycling) system was to be changed in such a way that you need not separate your waste at home at all, as this would be done on your behalf by a third party, how much would you be willing to pay for that service?

There is little difference in the mean WTP for the service for those who express significant environmental concern and those that do not. The reason for this is reflected in the fact that 65% of respondents who state a WTP of zero report that they would rather recycle themselves. Indeed, those respondents who state that they prefer to recycle themselves and report a WTP of zero tend to rank environmental concerns higher relative to five other concerns (international tensions, economic concerns, health concerns, social issues, personal safety) than the other two groups – i.e. those who state WTP of zero for other reasons, and those with WTP greater than zero. In addition, they are somewhat more likely to be members of or contributors to an environmental NGO (14.7%) than those who do not protest (13.9%).

Further analysis confirms that respondents attach a value to recycling, which is distinct from the potential implications of the service for the protection of the environment. Indeed, empirical analysis indicates that the "value" associated with recycling *per se* represents almost half the value of the stated WTP. Specifically, there are benefits associated with recycling oneself, and any proposed service which constrains the household's potential to engage in this activity needs to be assessed with care. Reasons for such a finding can be found in the sociological literature on "crowding out" in which particular policy programs or instruments can crowd out intrinsic motivations to provide the good voluntarily (see Frey, 1997; and Frey *et al.*, 2000). Such impacts can have an important effect on the relative effectiveness of different policy instruments.

4. Waste prevention

We have already seen that unit-based waste fees and recycling services can affect volumes of mixed waste generated and recycling rates. However, it is important to bear in mind that the effects of the two policies are quite different. While waste fees provide incentives for any strategy which avoids putting out waste for disposal (including prevention), recycling services only favour one strategy – i.e. recycling. Indeed, such a service could theoretically increase waste generation by subsidising waste management. As such, it is important to examine waste prevention.

Analysing waste prevention is, by nature, difficult. In effect, it is necessary to evaluate what waste would have been generated in the absence of a given policy intervention or some other factor. However, it is possible to obtain some indirect evidence by looking at purchases or use of products which are relatively less waste-intensive than substitutes. Figure 4.8 shows the proportion of households reporting that they always or often choose to use paper with recycled content, refillable containers and reusable shopping bags.

Figure 4.8. **Percentage of households choosing to use less waste-intensive products**

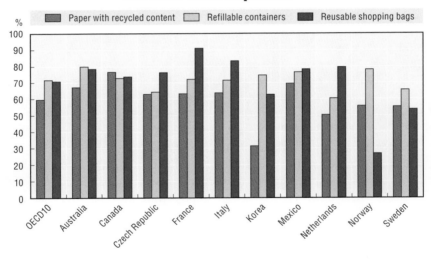

Source: OECD Project on Household Behaviour and Environmental Policy.

Overall, 60% of respondents always or often use paper with recycled content, 72% use refillable containers and 71% use reusable shopping bags. The proportion always or often using paper with recycled content varies from

31% in Korea to 77% in Canada. For refillable containers it varies from 60% in the Netherlands to 80% in Australia and, finally, for reusable shopping bags it varies from 27% in Norway to 91% in France.

Exploring the issue further, two further models were estimated, one based on whether refillable containers were ever used, and one involving an ordinal choice over regularity of use of refillable containers. The results in terms of demographics and economic variables differ for the two models. However, in both cases expressed concern for environmental matters has a positive impact. In addition, the presence of volume-based waste fees has a positive impact on the intensity of use. This highlights the importance of the point made above about the additional effect of waste fees relative to recycling collection services.

5. Conclusions

With regard to waste generation, results show that household waste generation is significantly affected by household attributes including gender, age, education, location of residence, and household size. As such, changes in household living patterns and demographic attributes will have an impact on waste generation. These factors need to be taken into account in waste management planning decisions. For instance, continued falls in household size will result in increased waste per capita. More importantly, the results indicate that a charge per unit of waste generated in volume terms has a significant impact on reducing waste generation. The effect of weight-based charging is not detected, although it must be borne in mind that the dependent variable is expressed in volume terms. In addition, stated concern for environmental matters reduces waste generation.

Results on the determinants of recycling indicate that the quality of recycling collection systems (*e.g.* door-to-door *versus* drop-off) has a significant effect on recycling rates. Unit pricing by volume also has an effect, but it is generally less important, and with greater variation of the impact across materials. Moreover, it has little effect on the decision to recycle or not, but does influence the level of recycling for those who already recycle.

To a certain extent, there is evidence that the two policies are substitutes rather than complements – at least from the perspective of their impact on recycling. However, it must be emphasised that unit waste fees provide incentives for any strategy that avoids putting out waste for disposal (including prevention), while collection or drop-off services for recyclable waste only favour one strategy – i.e. recycling. Indeed, such services could even theoretically increase waste generation by subsidising waste management overall. Further work on waste prevention is required to assess this question.

While it is not surprising to find that stated concern for the environment has a positive impact on recycling, it is interesting that social motivations which are distinct from explicitly environmental concerns also have an influence on recycling rates. This is confirmed in related work done on respondents' WTP for a paid recycling service. Some respondents preferred to recycle themselves (even if the impact on the environment was the same) rather than pay any amount for such a service. Such intrinsic and social motivations should be taken into account in policy design in order to minimise any "crowding out" of voluntary behaviour. More generally, it has implications for information-based campaigns.

And finally, in the area of waste it is particularly important to bear in mind administrative costs. For instance, while a drop-off scheme may be less effective in terms of increasing recycling rates than a door-to-door collection scheme, the latter is likely to be much more costly. The benefits may not be sufficient to warrant the additional cost. Similarly, targeting policies according to demographic characteristics may result in increased recycling, but the costs of targeting may be considerable.

Notes

1. Household waste represented 60% of municipal waste in the US, 67% in Japan, 65% in France, 75% in Austria, 49% in Finland, 58% in Hungary, 57% in Ireland, 53% in Norway, 69% in Poland, 67% in Swizerland (OECD, 2008).

2. Examining and rethinking the interaction among different types of motivation is gaining considerable attention in the field of economic psychology (Brekke et al., 2003; Frey, 1997; Thøgersen, 2003).

3. Food and garden waste is excluded since this is not common.

4. Although the estimated coefficient of the variable interacting the presence of unit pricing with the presence of recycling services is significant only for plastic, aluminium, and food recycling participation, the sign is negative for all materials but paper, thus suggesting that unit pricing and recycling services are not likely to be complementary policies.

References

Callan, S.J. and J.M. Thomas (1997), "The Impact of State and Local Policies on the Recycling Effort", *Eastern Economic Journal*, No. 23, pp. 411-423.

Dijkgraaf, E. and R.H.J.M. Gradus (2004), "Cost Savings in Unit-based Pricing of Household Waste: The Case of the Netherlands", *Resource and Energy Economics*, No. 26, pp. 353-371.

Ferrara, I. and P. Missios (2005), "Recycling and Waste Diversion Effectiveness: Evidence from Canada", *Environmental and Resource Economics*, No. 30, pp. 221-238.

Frey, B.S. (1997), *Not Just for the Money: An Economic Theory of Personal Motivation* (Cheltenham, UK: Edward Elgar, 1997).

Frey, Bruno S. and Jegen, Reto (2000). "Motivation Crowding Theory: A Survey of Empirical Evidence", *IEER Working Paper*, No. 26, Zurich; *CESifo Working Paper Series*, No. 245, available at SSRN: *http://ssrn.com/abstract=203330*.

OECD (2001), *OECD Environmental Outlook*, OECD, Paris.

OECD (2007), *Instrument Mixes for Environmental Policy*, Paris.

OECD (2008a), *Environmental Outlook to 2030*, OECD, Paris.

OECD (2008c), *OECD Environmental Data: COMPENDIUM 2006-2008*, OECD, Paris.

Skumatz, L.A. and D.J. Freeman (2007), *Pay as you Throw (PAYT) in the US: 2006 Update and Analyses*, report prepared for US EPA and SERA (Skumatz Economic Research Associates), SERA, Superior (CO).

Statistics Canada (2008), *Households and the Environment Survey*, Catalogue No. 11-526-X, ISSN 1913-5270, 2006.

Chapter 5

Personal Transport Choices

The transport sector is one of the major contributors to climate change. Personal transport also significantly contributes to local and regional air pollution with emission of pollutants such as nitrogen oxides and carbon monoxide. This chapter looks at the effects of different types of public policies influencing transport demand ranging from pricing measures, such as fuel taxes or financial incentives to buy "cleaner" vehicles, to car labelling or the provision of transport infrastructure. The main factors affecting car ownership, car use and car choice are analysed, as well as factors which encourage the use of public transport. The impact of the relative price of different means of transport on mode choice receives particular attention. The role of environmental "norms" on personal transport decisions is also considered, improving our understanding of how raising public awareness about the environmental effects of private car use can complement other policies.

1. Introduction

The transport sector is one of the major contributors to greenhouse gas emissions. The transport sector's contribution to climate change is around 20% of total emissions in countries which form part of the United Nations Framework Convention on Climate Change (UNFCCC).[1] Moreover, in 15 EU countries greenhouse gas emissions have been decreasing in recent years in all main sectors, with the exception of transport. In fact, from 1990 to 2006 they grew by 26% of which 90% were due to road transport (EEA, 2008). According to Stern (2007) "CO_2 emissions from transport are expected to more than double in the period to 2050", one of the fastest growing sectors.

Personal transport is also a significant contributor to local and regional air pollutants. Indeed, road traffic is the single most important source of nitrogen oxides, benzene and carbon monoxide in many countries. Lead emissions are decreasing in importance, but emissions of particulate matter (PM) are of increasing concern, and some of the health effects are summarised below. Secondary pollutants, such as nitrogen oxides and volatile organic compounds (VOCs) are also of concern, since they lead to the formation of tropospheric ozone (O_3).

While other transport modes (*e.g.* public transport) are not environmentally-benign, the impacts of personal car use per kilometre travelled, are by far the greatest. The environmental impacts of car use can be reduced by:

- reducing the number of vehicle kilometres driven and car-sharing;
- switching from car use to other transport modes which are less damaging;
- installing pollution control devices and improving combustion characteristics for petrol and diesel vehicles; and
- using alternative-fuelled vehicles (*e.g.* electric or hybrid vehicles).

To one extent or another the OECD project on "Environmental Policy and Household Behaviour" examined three of these four channels – with the third being the exception by looking at the policy, demographic and economic factors which affect people's decisions to adopt personal transport behaviour

Table 5.1. **Short-term and long-term effects of personal transport**

Pollutant	Short-term effects	Long-term effects
PM	• Increase in mortality. • Increase in hospital admissions. • Exacerbation of symptoms and increased use of therapy in asthma. • Cardiovascular effects. • Lung inflammatory reactions.	• Increase in lower respiratory symptoms. • Reduction in lung function in children and adults. • Increase in chronic obstructive pulmonary disease. • Increase in cardiopulmonary mortality and lung cancer. • Diabetes effects. • Increased risk for myocardial infarction. • Endothelial and vascular dysfunction. • Development of atherosclerosis.
O_3	• Increase in mortality. • Increase in hospital admissions. • Effects on pulmonary function. • Lung inflammatory reactions. • Respiratory symptoms. • Cardiovascular system effects.	• Reduced lung function. • Development of atherosclerosis. • Development of asthma. • Reduction in life expectancy.
NO_2	• Effects on pulmonary structure and function (asthmatics). • Increase in allergic inflammatory reactions. • Increase in hospital admissions. • Increase in mortality.	• Reduction in lung function. • Increased probability of respiratory symptoms. • Reproductive effects.

Source: Adapted from WHO (2004b, 2006).

which is more or less environmentally-damaging. There are three significant benefits of the project with respect to previous work in this area:

- Data have been collected across ten countries, allowing for significant variation in those demographic, socio-economic, spatial, and policy characteristics which are likely to affect mode choice.

- Data have been collected by mode (car, public transport, cycle, etc.) and travel purpose (commuting, shopping, etc.). Since different factors may affect mode choice for different travel purposes this is important.

- Data have been collected on both the "push" (*i.e.* fuel prices) and "pull" factors (*i.e.* transport infrastructure) which are likely to affect mode choice.

- Since the project as a whole covers a number of thematic areas, we are able to examine the role of environmental "norms" on personal transport decisions, an issue which has rarely been addressed empirically.

This chapter is based upon the report prepared for the OECD by Alejandro Guevara-Sangines and José Alberto Lara-Pulido (Universidad Iberoamericana, Mexico) on "Mode choice and public transport use" and the report prepared by Clotilde Bureau (formerly ENSAE), Nick Johnstone and Ysé Serret (OECD Secretariat) on "Car ownership and car use". The full technical reports are available at: *http://dx.doi.org/10.1787/9789264096875-en* and *www.oecd.org/environment/households/greeningbehaviour.*

Before proceeding to a discussion of the results of the OECD project the following section provides a brief literature review of previous work in this area. It is important to note that almost all of these studies cover a single country, and only a sub-set of the variables used in the OECD project. However, most draw upon "panel" data rather than a single cross-section which has important advantages for the analysis of certain personal transport decisions.

2. Literature review

Research on personal transport decisions has been focused on analysing the impact of several variables on households' transport choices. In this context, most studies try to explain households' decisions on transport mode choice, car ownership, and their use. However, there is a relatively small number of previous studies which examine decisions related to public transport, usually in terms of a substitute for car travel. Table 5.2 provides a summary table of the results.

The results show that, in general, the effects of economic and demographic variables are consistent with expectations. However, it is interesting to note that for many variables (*e.g.* income, age, gender) the signs are opposite for car ownership use and public transport use. With respect to the effect of city size and density this is also true, reflecting the economies of scale and density of public transport service provision.

As will be seen, the results of the work arising out of the OECD project are consistent with the results in the literature. However, there are three points to bear in mind:

- Relatively few studies look at the role of accessibility to public transport and attitudes toward the environment.
- Data coverage with respect to explanatory variables is often quite limited, particularly in the case of public transport.
- Moreover, the studies do not look at potential substitution with other modes (*e.g.* cycling or walking).

Before proceeding to a summary of the empirical results based on the OECD survey, the following sections provide some descriptive data on mode choice, car ownership and public transport use.

3. Mode choice

Figure 5.1 presents data on the aggregate figures for mode choice for four travel purposes (commuting, shopping, education, and visiting family and friends) for the full sample of responses from all ten countries. It is important to distinguish by travel purpose since quite different policy incentives may be needed in different cases. For instance, encouraging changes in mode choice for

Table 5.2. **Summary of results of previous studies**

Independent variable	Income	Age	Male	Education	HH size	Working (# No.)	Children (# No.)	Density/near CBD	Accessibility to public transport	Attitude to environment	Country
Car ownership											
Train (1980)	+				+			-			United States
Bhat and Koppelman (1993)	+			-			-#				Netherlands
Asensio et al. (2002)	+	+/-		+	+	+#					Spain
Dargay (2005a)	+	-		+	+	+	+0-		-		EU14
Simma and Axhausen (2004)			+				-#				Austria
Abreu e Silva et al. (2006)	+	-	+		+	+#		-	-		Portugal
Giuliano and Dargay (2006)	+	-			+		+	-	-		United States/ United Kingdom
Nolan (2002)	+	+	+	+	+	+	+#	+#	-		Ireland
OECD Survey	**+**	**+**	**+**	**0**	**+**	**+**	**+**	**+**	**-**	**-**	**OECD10**
Car use											
De Jong (1996)	+	-	+	+	+	+		-			Netherlands
Abreu e Silva et al. (2006)	+	-	+		+	+		-			Portugal
Feng et al. (2005)	+	-	+	+	+	+/#	##				United States
Fullerton et al. (2005)	+	-	+	-	0	+/-	+				Japan
Steg et al. (2001)	+	+/-	+	+	-		-			-	Netherlands
Johansson-Stenman (2002)	+	+	+								Sweden
Dargay and Hanly (2004)	+	+/-	+		+	+		-			United Kingdom
Asensio et al. (2000)	+	+/-		+	+	+#	+				Spain
Nolan (2002)	+	0	+	0	+	+			-		Ireland
Simma and Axhausen (2004)			+			+	-#				Austria
Golob and Hensher (1998)	?		+/-	-	-	-(F)#	+(F)			-	Australia
Dargay (2005)	+	+	0	0	+	+	0	-	-		United Kingdom
OECD Survey	**+**	**+/-**	**+**	**0**	**+**	**+**	**0**	**-**	**+**	**-**	**OECD10**

Table 5.2. **Summary of results of previous studies** (cont.)

Independent variable	Income	Age	Male	Education	HH size	Working (# No.)	Children (# No.)	Density/near CBD	Accesibility to public transport	Attitude to environment	Country
Public transport use											
Abreu e Silva *et al.* (2006)	–	+	–								Portugal
Johansson-Stenman (2002)	–	–/+	–	+						0	Sweden
Golob and Hensher (1998)	+	–/+	–	–+/			–			+	Australia
Dieleman *et al.* (2002)	–			–			–				Netherlands
OECD Survey	**–**	**–/+**	**0**	**+**	**0**	**–**	**–**	**+**	**+**	**+**	**OECD10**

Source: OECD (2008b), *Household Behaviour and the Environment: Reviewing the Evidence*, OECD, Paris.

Figure 3.13. **Households installing energy-efficiency-rate appliances in the last 10 years by the importance of environmental benefits in encouraging households to reduce energy consumption**

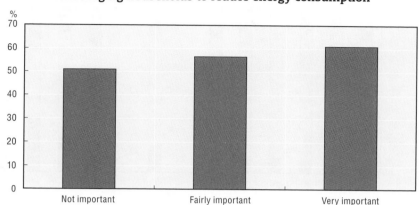

Source: OECD Project on Household Behaviour and Environmental Policy.

4. The demand for renewable energy

The survey responses provide information on households' demand for renewable energy by asking respondents if they take special measures to buy renewable energy from their electricity provider and how much they would be willing-to-pay to use "green" energy.

Taking special action to buy "green" energy or to invest in renewable energy

Just under 20% of households state that they "take special measures to buy renewable energy from their service providers".[4] Results show variations across countries with the Netherlands and Korea having the highest percentages of respondents stating this to be the case. As expected, countries with a large percentage of hydroelectric energy in their standard fuel mix, like Canada and Norway, report low percentages. It is interesting to note that almost 20% of the people surveyed do not know if they take special measures to buy renewable energy from their electricity provider, suggesting that improved information campaigns have a role to play (see Figure 3.14).

The results also indicate that those who invest in renewable energy technologies are different in some dimensions from those who have chosen not to. Information about investment in renewable energy equipment in the past 10 years collected in the survey shows that an "investor" is more likely to be: Italian, Norwegian or Korean (and less likely to be a Canadian); a man; living in a detached house; a member of an environmental organisation, and

Figure 3.14. **Taking special measures to buy green energy**

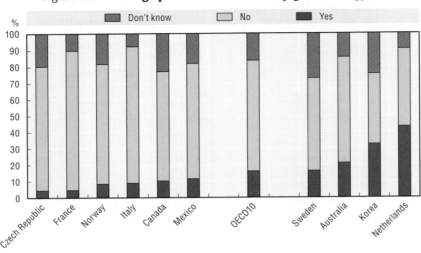

Source: OECD Project on Household Behaviour and Environmental Policy.

to have also installed energy efficiency equipment (*e.g.* a condensing boiler). Because only about 5% of the sample has invested in renewable energy equipment, these results need to be interpreted with caution.

An econometric analysis of renewable energy demand drivers was undertaken. The results indicate that a respondent who is active in the market for renewable energy is more likely to be active in an environmental organisation and to be "environmentally concerned". The survey confirms that general attitude towards the environment influences demand for renewable energy. This is consistent with earlier studies showing membership in environmental organisations to be an important factor in the residential market for renewable energy.

Active respondents on the renewable energy market are more often found to be conscious of energy costs when renting or buying their residence. Besides, when looking at gender, women have a higher estimated probability of not taking special measures to buy renewable energy from their electricity provider and the number of children in the households seems to matter as well. In addition, there is some indication that the age group 45 to 55 has a significantly higher probability of saying that they do not take special measures. It is worth noting that there are significant differences between several countries unrelated to the sets of explanatory variables.

Figure 5.1. **Mode choice by travel purpose (full sample)**

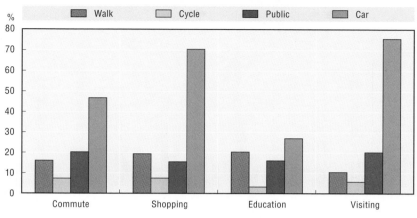

Source: OECD Project on Household Behaviour and Environmental Policy.

habitual (*e.g.* commuting to and from work) and episodic (*e.g.* visiting family and friends) travel may require different policy levers. Similarly, encouraging change in mode choice for travel purposes which are more "cumbersome" (*e.g.* shopping) is often linked with cultural habits and land use patterns.

Car travel is the most common mode for all travel purposes except education. Car travel is used intensively for "visiting friends and family". It is notable that cars are the most common mode for shopping, with 70% responding that they use this mode regularly. The use of public transport is relatively uniform across different travel purposes.

Are there differences across countries? Due to its relative importance in total travel, Figure 5.2 gives the percentages for commuting to and from work disaggregated by country. The use of the car is the most common mode in all countries except Korea, where public transport is most common. Australia is the country with the greatest share of trips made by car, and with one of the smallest shares of trips by bicycle. Public transport comes second in most countries. Cycling to and from work is much more common in the Netherlands (and to a lesser extent Sweden and Norway) than elsewhere.

Figure 5.3 provides the same information for shopping, a travel purpose for which significant efforts in a number of OECD countries have been made to bring about changes in mode choice (*i.e.* restrictions on out-of-town shopping centres). However, even more than is the case for commuting, travelling to shopping facilities is done most frequently by car. Walking is relatively common, often ranking second in importance (Canada, France, Italy, the Czech Republic, Sweden, Norway) ahead of public transport. Once again, cycling is common in the Netherlands, and to a lesser extent Sweden. Empirical work

Figure 5.2. **Mode choice for commuting by country**

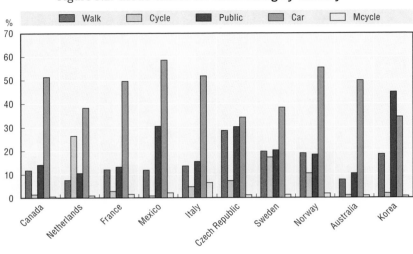

Source: OECD Project on Household Behaviour and Environmental Policy.

Figure 5.3. **Mode choice for shopping by country**

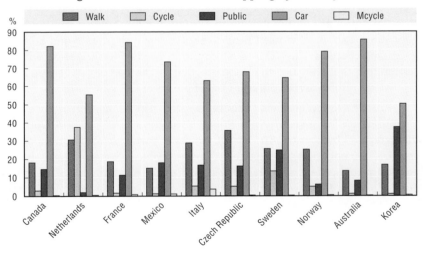

Source: OECD Project on Household Behaviour and Environmental Policy.

indicates that spatial characteristics and environmental concern are important factors in this choice. However, even taking such factors into account, there is important "residual" variation which is explained by the country in question, and thus perhaps attributable to cultural characteristics and cycling infrastructure. Data provided below confirm the importance of the latter point.

In general, the share of trips associated with educational activities is more evenly distributed across different modes. The pattern of trips for sporting and cultural activities (not reported) indicates that an important proportion of trips for these purposes are made by modes other than the car. However, at least in the former case (sports) this could indicate that walking and cycling are considered as an activity in and of itself, rather than a mode of transport.

With some exceptions, the overall picture that emerges is that car travel is the most common mode, and that public transport and walking are the second most common choices, having similar shares in several cases. However, in the case of commuting, empirical work has shown that the choice between these two is largely a function of distance travelled. Cycling is the least commonly used travel mode option. However, it is the area in which variation is the greatest, and thus potentially one in which increased use can be induced.

Despite these generalities, differences by country are significant. For example, in South Korea a very different pattern is observed: the importance of trips by public transport is the same or greater than the importance of car trips. Only in the Netherlands, Sweden, the Czech Republic and Norway does cycling appear to be an even moderately important mode of transport.

4. Car ownership, choice and use

Car ownership is a "discrete" decision, and one which has significant influence on all subsequent choices of mode for different travel purposes. The decision not to own a car can be seen as a decision to restrict mode choice. This is not true of other modes (except perhaps cycling in the absence of a public services such as Velib). As such, it is important to look at the decision to own (and use) a car in some detail.

Respondents were asked to report the number of cars their household owned. In total, 13.7% of the respondents reported having no car, 46.1% one car, and 31.6% two cars. Very few households reported having more than two cars. The mean number of cars in the different country samples is presented in Table 5.3 below. (For corroboration of this data see *www.oecd.org/environment/households*.)

Those households that did not own a car were requested to indicate the primary reason why they did not do so. Figure 5.4 summarises the responses. As expected, affordability is the main factor, but it is revealing that "environmental" concerns rank so low. Indeed, there is little correlation between respondents' declared concern for the environment and car ownership, indicating that if this factor plays a role it is relatively less important than the other factors (*e.g.* income) which are likely to affect car ownership.

Alternative car technologies such as hybrid, electric and (in some cases) biofuel vehicles are a potential means of reducing greenhouse gas emissions and emission of local air pollutants. In the survey, respondents were

Table 5.3. **Mean number of cars per household and per household member**

	Mean per household	Standard deviation	Mean per capita	Standard deviation	Observations
Canada	2.424	.910	.711	.267	984
Netherlands	1.997	.730	.656	.265	1 010
France	2.505	.794	.756	.278	1 055
Mexico	2.558	1.040	.590	.303	969
Italy	2.720	.861	.715	.249	1 397
Czech Republic	2.226	.892	.598	.264	694
Sweden	1.985	.847	.654	.308	987
Norway	2.410	.873	.733	.304	985
Australia	2.629	.931	.731	.264	986
Korea	2.152	.705	.489	.200	963

Note: Standard deviation shows how much variation or "dispersion" there is from the *mean*.
Source: OECD Project on Household Behaviour and Environmental Policy.

Figure 5.4. **Stated reasons for not owning a car**

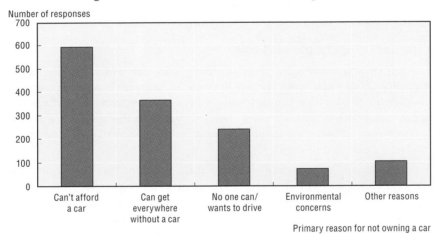

Source: OECD Project on Household Behaviour and Environmental Policy.

requested to provide information on the fuel type of their vehicle. The percentage of respondents in the total sample who reported having an alternative fuel car as their main car is very small (less than 6%), and it mainly corresponds to people owning a LPG (liquefied petroleum gas) car (87%).

While these results may suggest that market penetration of such types of vehicles is still limited, it could also be due to the fact that alternative fuel vehicles may be used as a second car rather than as a main car. Indeed, the average number of cars owned is higher for people owning hybrid vehicles. In addition, people having LPG or hybrid vehicles are more concentrated in suburban and urban areas. One could assume that infrastructure associated with alternative fuel vehicles is more developed in more concentrated areas. There are also more people in the highest income decile in the sub-sample of people owning a hybrid vehicle than for people having a conventional fuel vehicle. Finally, membership of an environmental organisation is positively correlated with the ownership of an alternative fuel vehicle. As market penetration increases it will be possible to look at these issues in greater depth.

For car owners, mean weekly (personal) driving distances are given in Figure 5.5 below. There is a negative correlation between the index of environmental attitudes on the one hand, and both car ownership and average weekly kilometers driven amongst car-owning households on the other hand. The importance of such attitudes relative to economic, demographic and policy factors is discussed below.

Figure 5.5. **Number of kilometres driven per week by respondents in car-owning households**

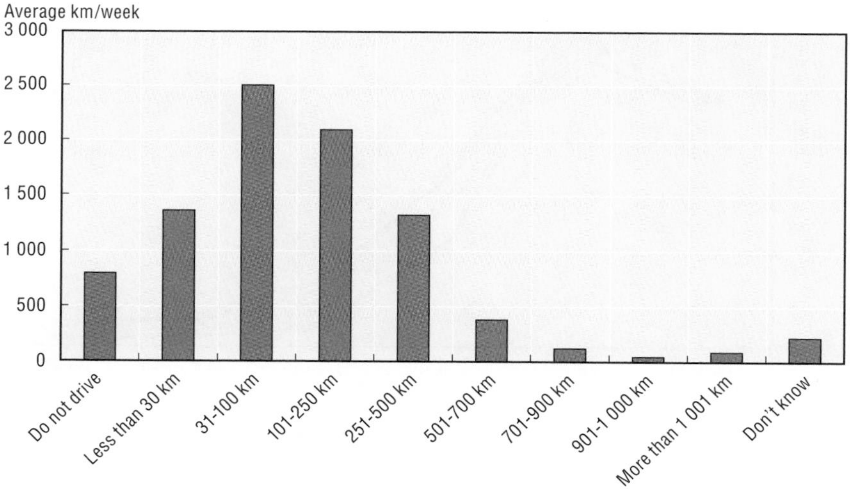

Source: OECD Project on Household Behaviour and Environmental Policy.

5. Public transport accessibility and use

In order to bring about less environmentally-damaging personal transport patterns, one of the greatest challenges is to encourage the substitution of car travel for public transport. In order to understand what motivates people to use (or not use) public transport, data were collected on accessibility. Specifically, respondents were requested to indicate "how far is your primary residence from the public transport/station which is most convenient for your daily commute?"

Respondents could indicate whether it was: less than five minutes; 5 to 15 minutes; 16 to 30 minutes; 31 to 45 minutes; 46 minutes to an hour; and over 1 hour.

Differences across countries can be seen in Figure 5.6 below. Since responses for urban and rural households are likely to differ to such a great extent, the figure only includes "urban" households. Much of the variation can be seen with respect to those who live less than 15 minutes from the most convenient stop. The Netherlands and Norway stand out, followed by France and Italy. At the other extreme are Mexico and Australia.

Figure 5.6. **Distance (in minutes) to most convenient public transport stop**

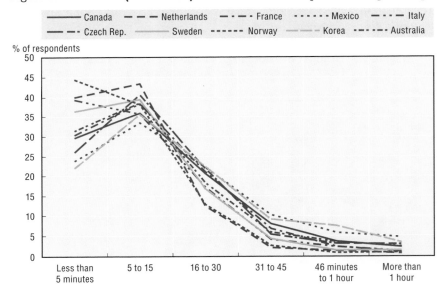

Source: OECD Project on Household Behaviour and Environmental Policy.

The relationship between access to a public transport stop and average driving distance is given in Figure 5.7. There is a marked tendency for respondents with less convenient access to public transport to drive more than others. However, this difference only appears to become particularly marked once public transport becomes very inconvenient (> 30 minutes). The mean weekly driving distance for households is 126 kilometres for households within 15 minutes of a public transport stop, rising to 163 kilometres for those in the range 15-30 minutes, and 225 kilometres for those greater than 30 minutes.

The empirical results reported below indicate that there is a significant difference between the effect of being within 5 and 15 minutes of a public transport stop in terms of car ownership and use. Moreover, above fifteen

Figure 5.7. **Convenience of access (minutes) to public transport
and weekly vehicle kilometres driven**

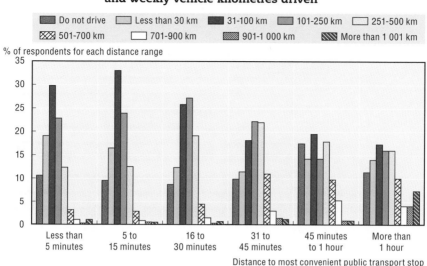

Source: OECD Project on Household Behaviour and Environmental Policy.

minutes there is no discernible impact. However, convenience of access is only one attribute of public transport amongst many and it is therefore necessary to determine precisely those factors which are likely to induce greater use of public transport if policy makers are to encourage mode switching. In Figure 5.8 the average ranking of the effect of different aspects of public transport are given. Rapidity is an important factor in most countries. However, in some countries other factors are more important – *i.e.* personal security in Mexico, reliability in Sweden and convenience in France. Significantly, for all ten countries personal security is ranked (on average) higher by women than men.

In addition to public transport, cycling is of course a potential substitute for personal car travel. Figure 5.9 presents the relationship between the frequency of cycling as a travel mode for different travel purposes and the percentage of respondents that stated that "more and better cycle paths" would encourage them to travel by car less often. There is a pronounced negative relationship (correlation = –0.54) indicating that those countries in which cycling is not common would see significant increase in the choice of this mode with greater investment in cycling infrastructure. As expected, this relationship is even stronger for the urban population (correlation = –0.60).

Figure 5.8. **Influence of improvements in public transport on increasing use**

1 = least important and 5 = most important

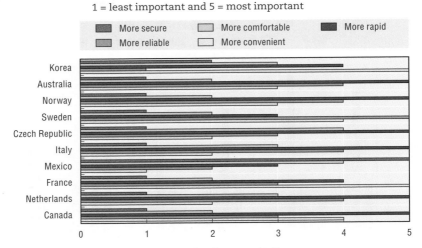

Source: OECD Project on Household Behaviour and Environmental Policy.

Figure 5.9. **Cycling infrastructure and frequency of use**

% of respondents stating that "more and better cycle paths" would incite them to reduce car use

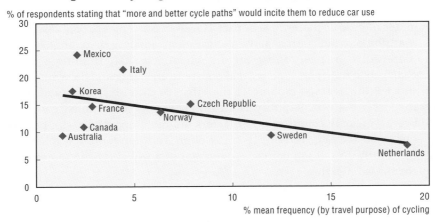

Source: OECD Project on Household Behaviour and Environmental Policy.

6. The determinants of mode choice

Car ownership and use

What factors are encouraging households to own and use their cars? While the correlations presented in Sections 3 and 4 indicate that environmental attitudes and access to public transport have an impact on car ownership and use, the empirical evidence indicates that a large number of other factors are at play. For instance, based upon a review of previous literature in this area

110

(summarised above), a number of economic and demographic variables are important, including income, operating costs of the vehicle, age of the respondent, household size and composition (*e.g.* number of children), location of residence, and employment status.

Given the large number of factors involved, econometric models are required to try and answer this question. In order to obtain reliable results, the two decisions (ownership and use) were estimated together.[2] The results are largely consistent with the existing literature and expectations.

Income has a positive and significant effect on both car ownership and driving distance,[3] as does employment (whether full-time or part-time). In terms of demographics, men are more likely to own cars, and to drive greater distances. Car ownership increases with age, but the sign on the square of age is negative and significant, suggesting that the effect of age decreases after a certain point. The relationship between age and car use is the same. Residing in an urban area decreases ownership and use, as expected. And finally, having children five years of age or less in the household increases the likelihood of car ownership.

Figure 5.10 summarises the results for the main variables of more policy-relevance. The results are expressed in terms of elasticities. Firstly, the proxy variable for fuel price has the expected negative effect on driving distance, although the effect is relatively small.[4] This supports more descriptive evidence in which respondents indicated that on average a 20% increase in fuel prices would reduce their consumption by approximately 7%-8%.

Figure 5.10. **Effects of fuel prices, transport accessibility and environmental attitudes on car ownership and use**

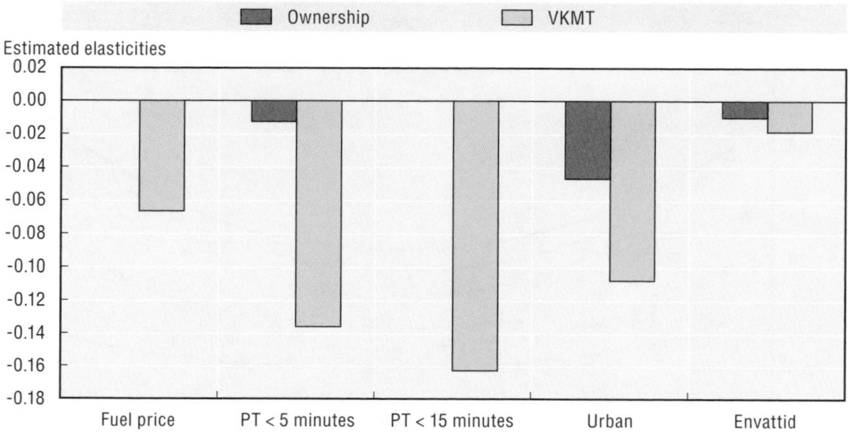

Source: OECD Project on Household Behaviour and Environmental Policy.

The index variable reflecting "environmental norms" has a negative effect on car ownership, but not on driving distance (the coefficient is insignificant) – *i.e.* environmental norms affect the decision to own a car, but not the use of the car if there is one in the household. Another interesting result relates to the effect of access to public transport, with a negative and significant sign on car use if the household lives within either 5 or 15 minutes of a public transport stop. However, for ownership the effect only holds if the household lives within five minutes of a public transport stop.

Since increased use of public transport is likely to be the most effective way to reduce the environmental impacts associated with personal car use, it is interesting to note that 35% of respondents state that they would drive their cars less if public transport was cheaper. However, the likely magnitude of such a response was examined in more detail through the use of a set of more sophisticated models[5] which estimated mode choice for the different travel purposes.

The effect of income on the odds of commuting by public transport relative to commuting by car is negative. That is to say, as income rises, there are less chances of choosing public transport. The predicted probabilities when travelling to undertake professional or educational activities are the highest. In contrast, when shopping, these probabilities are the lowest. With respect to age, a life-cycle effect is found.[6] Younger and older people have higher probabilities of commuting by public transport than middle-aged ones. For all destinations the minimum probability of choosing public transport is at the age of 48 years old, approximately (see Figure 5.11).

Figure 5.11. **Age (predicted probabilities of commuting by public transport)**

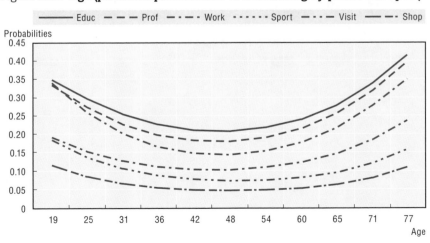

Source: OECD Project on Household Behaviour and Environmental Policy.

For almost all travel purposes the number of adults in the household has a weak effect on mode choice, with the exception of educational activities. There is not a statistically significant difference between females and males in terms of mode choice. The number of children decreases the probability of choosing public transport; however, a significant effect is only found when travelling to accomplish educational activities and when visiting family and friends.

Our findings are consistent with past studies that indicate that people in urban municipalities and/or not living in detached houses have greater odds to use public transport relative to commuting by car. The effect of a dummy variable which is equal to one when there is not a public transport station in reasonable proximity to the residence indicates that instead of walking or cycling people prefer to commute by car. The effect is greatest for shopping and commuting – indicating that these "habitual" travel purposes are most affected by the absence of accessible public transport.

The index of environmental attitudes was also included in the models. Environmental norms do have an influence on mode choice for commuting to and from work, educational activities, and leisure activities (sport and visiting family and friends). The stronger the norms the greater the probability that public transport or cycling will be chosen over car travel. The effect on cycling is greater than the effect on public transport for commuting, visiting family and friends and sporting activities (see Figure 5.12). It is interesting that mode choice for shopping is not affected by environmental norms (the bars are in light to reflect the statistical insignificance of the variables).

Figure 5.12. **Effect of environmental norms on mode choice (relative to car travel)**

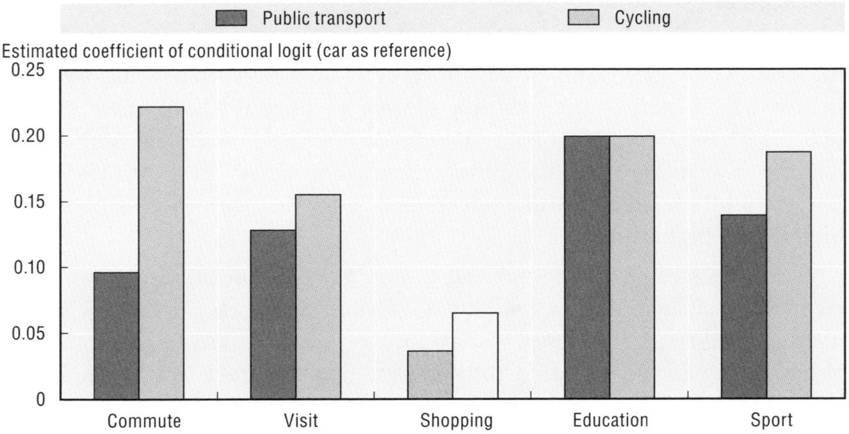

Source: OECD Project on Household Behaviour and Environmental Policy.

To capture "fixed" effects by country a set of dummies were included in estimations. Thus, taking into account all differences between countries and respondents (*i.e.* spatial characteristics, economic factors, etc.) there are still country-specific effects which indicate that:

- Respondents in the Czech Republic and France have the largest probabilities of travel by foot (with the exception when destination is shopping).

- Respondents in Mexico have the highest probabilities of commuting by car for five of six travel purposes (with the exception of sports and cultural activities).

- Respondents in South Korea have the highest probabilities of commuting by public transport independently of travel purpose.

- Respondents in the Netherlands reflect the highest probabilities of cycling independent of travel purpose.

Another systematic difference is found with respect to regional effects. In general, willingness to commute by foot or by public transport is greatest in: New South Wales and Victoria (Australia), Ontario and Quebec (Canada), Ile de France (France), North West and South regions (Italy), North-west region and Prague (the Czech Republic), Federal District and State of Mexico (Mexico), Oslo (Norway), and Gavleborg and Gotland (Sweden). With these results, it seems that regional differences come mainly from accessibility to public transport and the size of the municipality.

7. Conclusions and policy implications

This study has sought to cast further light on the determinants of personal transport choices. In particular, data were collected on mode choice, car ownership, fuel choice, public transport accessibility and a number of other relevant factors.

While the OECD collected some data on the ownership of alternative-fuelled vehicles, ownership is not sufficient to draw any firm conclusions on the factors which increase penetration. Moreover, since much of environmental policy with respect to personal transport has focussed on the use of incentives (pricing, regulatory, information) to encourage substitution from personal car use to public transport this chapter has primarily summarised the work undertaken in this area.

It is clear that demographic (*e.g.* age, gender, household composition) economic (*e.g.* income, employment status) and structural factors (*e.g.* location of residence) affect the choice between these two modes. These factors can be considered exogenous – and thus not subject to direct influence through environmental policy. However, an understanding of their role is important in assessing the likely impacts of different policies on personal transport choices. Moreover, in the longer term some of these factors – *e.g.* location of residence in relation to destination for different travel purposes – are subject to policy influence. Efforts to discourage out-of-town shopping and urban sprawl can be seen in this light, and the results of the OECD project indicate that they will reduce car use significantly.

From a policy perspective it is hardly surprising to find that the relative price of different modes has an influence on mode choice. While the variable used in the empirical work to reflect the relative cost of car use is far from ideal, the results confirm that changing the relative cost of the two modes will influence personal transport choices. This result is supported by the stated responses of respondents to the survey with respect to a number of questions. For instance, 35% of respondents indicated that they would drive their cars less if public transport was cheaper. Similarly, respondents indicated that on average a 20% increase in fuel prices would reduce their consumption by approximately 7%-8%.

While prices matter, given the nature of personal transport decisions they may not suffice. In order to be discouraged from using the car, it is important that there be a substitute mode available. The results indicate clearly that improving the accessibility of public transport will reduce car ownership and use, and encourage the use of public transport. However, "accessibility" needs to be carefully defined – above 15 minutes there is no discernible impact, and below five minutes the impact on car use is considerably greater.

More generally, public transport service quality is likely to decrease car use and increase public transport use. While rapidity and convenience are cited as being important additional factors in all countries, the other factors which also matter differ by country – i.e. personal security in Mexico, comfort in the Czech Republic. Improved reliability is important in Sweden, but not at all in Korea. This is instructive for policy design – the factors which will encourage people to use public transport vary by country.

In addition, a better cycling infrastructure is also likely to reduce car use, particularly in those countries where use of this mode is limited at present. Given the relative costs associated with developing a cycling infrastructure this may be a relatively efficient policy option in those countries in which the frequency of use of this mode is limited at present (e.g. Mexico, Korea, Australia). However, the results indicate that substitution possibilities vary greatly by travel purpose. Shopping seems to pose a particular challenge for obvious logistical reasons. However, the extent of variation across countries is instructive, and indicates that significant substitution can be encouraged in some countries.

Above and beyond the effects of factors such as price and infrastructure, it is clear that the attitude of respondents toward environmental issues has an effect on personal transport decisions. This effect is stronger with respect to car ownership than use, indicating that concern for the environment has a greater impact on "discrete" choices. The effect of environmental "norms" also varies by travel purpose. They do affect travel for commuting and educational purposes. These results indicate that a soft policy effectively influencing people's beliefs and attitudes to the environment would have a positive impact on substituting their car for an alternative mode.

Overall the results indicate the importance of looking at mode choice and travel purpose together. In addition, it can be concluded that a mix of push-pull instruments is required in order to encourage transport choices which are less environmentally-damaging. Increasing the cost of driving and accessibility to public transport must go hand-in-hand. Furthermore, a combination of "hard" policies (e.g. taxes and regulations) and "soft" policies (i.e. which inform people's attitudes) is required to induce mode switching. And finally, some policies will have a greater impact on decisions which relate to discrete decisions (e.g. car ownership), while others will have a greater impact on everyday decisions (e.g. mode choice for a particular travel purpose).

Notes

1. These countries are those included in "Annex 1" of the Convention, which include the industrialised countries that were members of the OECD in 1992, and some countries with economies in transition, including the Russian Federation, the Baltic States, and several Central and Eastern European States.

2. Specifically, a selection equation is estimated, in which a probit model is estimated to determine car ownership. The results of this are then used to estimate driving distance using ordinary least squares.

3. Respondents were requested to report their combined annual household after-tax income with respect to twelve different income brackets, differentiated by country. This was transformed into a continuous variable by taking the mid-point of the ten intermediate ranges. The values for the bottom and top brackets were determined by fitting a polynomial. The values were then converted into euros on the basis of nominal exchange rates, giving 120 potential values (10 countries by 12 brackets).

4. This is not strictly a fuel price elasticity since data was not collected on actual prices paid. Respondents reported their monthly expenditures on fuel, and a proxy for the fuel price was obtained by dividing fuel expenditures by monthly vehicle kilometres driven. However, since this value will also reflect a number of factors which are not accounted for (e.g. vehicle fuel efficiency, driving conditions, etc.), the estimated coefficients of this variable should not be interpreted as fuel price elasticities.

5. Specifically, conditional logit models were estimated, which allows for the substitution between modes to be tested directly.

6. This approach permits us to observe both marginal effects and predicted probabilities. When a coefficient is not significant it is indicated by a dashed line/bar. Probabilities were predicted for all values that a certain variable can take and fixing all other variables at their mean. In the case of dichotomous variables the change on predicted probability is presented instead of probabilities. Also, fixed effects by country are presented with predicted probability for each destination.

References

Abreu e Silva, J. de, T.F. Golob and K.G. Goulias (2006), "The Effects of Land Use Characteristics on Residence Location and Travel Behavior of Urban Adult Workers", paper presented at the 85th Transport Research Board Annual Meeting, Washington DC.

Asensio, J., A. Matas and J.L. Raymond (2002), "Petrol Expenditure and Redistributive Effects of its Taxation in Spain", *Transportation Research Part A*, Vol. 37, pp. 49-69.

Bhat, C.R. and F.S. Koppelman (1993), "An Endogenous Switching Simultaneous Equation System of Employment, Income and Car Ownership", *Transportation Research Part A*, Vol. 27(5), pp. 49-69.

Dargay, J. (2005), "L'automobile en Europe : Changement de comportements d'équipement et d'usage", *Étude spécifique britannique*, final report to ADEME, August.

Dargay, J. and M. Hanly (2004), "Land Use and Mobility", Proceedings of the World Conference on Transport Research, Istanbul, Turkey.

de Jong, G. (1996), "A Disaggregate Model System of Vehicle Holding Duration, Type Choice and Use", *Transportation Research Part B*, Vol. 30(4), pp. 245-324.

Dieleman, F., M. Dijst and G. Burghouwt (2002), "Urban Form and Travel Behaviour: Micro-level Household Attributes and Residential Context", *Urban Studies*, Vol. 39(3), pp. 507-552.

EEA (2008), *Greenhouse Gas Emission Trends and Projections in Europe 2008: Tracking Progress Towards Kyoto Targets*, Copenhagen, Denmark.

Feng, Y., D. Fullerton and L. Gan (2005), "Vehicle Choices, Miles Driven and Pollution Policies", *Working Paper*, No. 11553, National Bureau of Economic Research, available at *www.nber.org/papers/w11553*.

Fullerton, D. and A. Wolverton (2005), "The Two-Part Instrument in a Second-Best World", *Journal of Public Economics*, Vol. 89, pp. 1961-1975.

Giuliano, G. and J. Dargay (2006), "Car Ownership, Travel and Land Use: A Comparison of the US and Great Britain", *Transportation Research Part A*, Vol. 40, pp. 106-124.

Golob, T.F. and D.A. Hensher (1998), "Greenhouse Gas Emissions and Australian Commuters' Attitudes and Behaviour Concerning Abatement Policies and Personal Involvement", *Transportation Research Part D*, Vol. 3(1), pp. 1-19.

Johansson-Stenman, O. (2002), "Estimating Individual Driving Distance by Car and Public Transport Use in Sweden", *Applied Economics*, Vol. 34(8), pp. 959-967.

Nolan, A. (2002), *The Determinants of Urban Households' Transport Decisions: A Microeconometric Study Using Irish Data*, No. 150, Royal Economic Society Annual Conference 2002, available at *http://repec.org/res2002/Nolan_A.pdf*.

Simma, A. and K.W. Axhausen (2004), "Interactions between Travel Behaviour, Accessibility and Personal Characteristics: The Case of the Upper Austria Region", *European Journal of Transport and Infrastructure Research*, No. 3, pp. 147-162.

Steg, L., K. Geurs and M. Ras (2001), "The Effects of Motivational Factors on Car Use: A Multidisciplinary Approach", *Transportation Research Part A*, Vol. 35, pp. 789-806.

Stern, N. (2007), *The Economics of Climate Change: The Stern Review*, Cambridge, Cambridge University Press.

Train, K. (1980), "A Structured Logit Model of Auto Ownership and Mode Choice", *Review of Economic Studies*, Vol. 47(2), pp. 357-370.

WHO (2004b), *Health Aspects of Air Pollution – Results from the WHO Project "Systematic Review of Health Aspects of Air Pollution in Europe"*, WHO, Copenhagen.

WHO (2006), *WHO Air Quality Guidelines: Global Update 2005*, WHO.

Chapter 6

Organic Food Consumption

Food production and consumption is exerting increasing pressure on the environment, in particular through water, energy, pesticide and fertiliser use. This chapter looks at the impact of instruments directly targeting consumer choice concerning organic food consumption, such as organic labelling and raising awareness through public information campaigns. It provides a better understanding of the main motivations for consuming organic food. The importance of private considerations, like health concerns, is compared to the role of environmental motivations in households' decision to consume organic food. The chapter also examines how much more households are willing to pay for organic food products compared to conventional ones.

1. Introduction

Food production and consumption is exerting increasing pressure on the environment, in particular through water, energy, pesticide and fertiliser use. A number of factors influence food consumption and its impacts, such as population dynamics and demographic changes (urbanisation, household size). Food consumption is also driven by rising per capita incomes. Global per capita food consumption (kcal/person/day) is projected to rise to 3 050 kcal in 2030, compared to 2 800 for 1997-99 (OECD, 2008a).

In response to growing worldwide food demand, changes in food consumption patterns and reductions of their environmental impacts are receiving a lot of attention. In this context, a number of quality-differentiated products have emerged on the market to meet consumers' demand for more environmentally-friendly food products, ranging from organic food products to pesticide-free products or production systems using integrated pest management principles (IPM). Europe is the main market for organic products with an annual growth between 10-15%, together with North America (IFOAM, 2007).

Various types of policies are available to governments to facilitate the development of the organic market. This project focuses on the demand side and the impact of policy options to enhance organic food supply – such as subsidising organic production – is outside the scope of this study. The survey looks at the impact of instruments directly targeting consumer choice concerning organic food consumption, such as the provision of information (*e.g.* organic labelling, raising awareness). Economic instruments may also be used such as price subsidies for organic products, although this is not common.

Therefore, public policies on the demand-side mainly seek to address a situation of imperfect information or asymmetric information between consumers and producers and to help the market function better by delivering reliable information to the consumers. When making choices about environmentally-friendly food products, such as organic food, it is important to recognise that some aspects of product quality, like taste, are only detectable after consumption while other characteristics, like environmental aspects, cannot be determined by the consumer with any degree of precision at all.[1]

Organic food labelling is one of the key policy measures aimed at allowing consumers to make more informed choices. Labels generally signal that organic agricultural practices are followed in the production process.

Depending on the definition used, fewer chemicals (*e.g.* pesticides, fertilisers), if any, may be used. All ten countries surveyed have organic labels at the national level and in some cases, a supranational label, the EU organic logo for instance, is also displayed on products.

Organic food labelling may be implemented by governments directly. It may also be implemented by producers or retailers, but the government still has an important regulatory role in order to protect consumers from false claims. Requirements vary across countries and generally involve a set of production standards. Studies indicate that the effectiveness of labelling depends on how reliable the certification system is at ensuring that the practices adopted at the farm level are in line with the claims made on the label (OECD, 2008b). One recent example is Canada's new organic food certification standard, introduced in 2009, requiring mandatory certification for agricultural products represented as organic in import, export and inter-provincial trade.

Raising consumer awareness through public information and education campaigns is another key measure available to governments to promote organic food products. Organising promotion campaigns to inform consumers is a major component of the European Action Plan for Organic Food and Farming.[2] EU-wide promotion programmes have been launched, in addition to national campaigns in countries such as the Czech Republic, France, Italy and the Netherlands.[3]

Better understanding of the main drivers of consumer's behaviour towards organic food is important for effective policy design. This is one objective of the OECD survey. Drawing upon observations from over 10 000 households in ten OECD countries, the survey provides insights into key issues including:

- *Main motivations for consuming organic food.* As expected, high prices appear as the most important factor restricting market share. Results confirm the importance of private considerations, like health concerns, in households' decisions to consume organic food. Public considerations (*i.e.* protection of the environment or animal welfare) also have an influence.

- *Role of labelling at inducing organic food consumption.* Identification of relevant labels does not appear to be an issue in most countries surveyed, and almost half of respondents recognised organic labels, although with some variation across countries. Trust in labelling and certification seems to be key in the motivation to consume organic.

- *Differences in organic consumption behaviour across different household groups.* In line with previous evidence, only a small number of socio-demographic characteristics (*e.g.* age, education) are found to have a significant influence on organic food consumption. However, the factors which affect the choice to consume organic food at all or not seem to differ from those factors which affect relative consumption levels for those who purchase at least some organic food products.

- *Willingness-to-pay more for organic food products compared to conventional ones.* The survey results indicate that consumers are generally not willing to pay more than 15% relative to conventional food products, whatever the food category. As expected, those concerned with the environment and those perceiving significant health benefits from organic food are willing to pay higher premia. Amongst the factors that explain differences in WTP is the ease of identification and comprehension of organic labelling. Consumers who do not trust existing certification systems are not willing to pay much for organics.

This chapter is based on the report prepared for the OECD by the Italian research team lead by Stefano Boccaletti (Catholic University, Italy). The full technical report is available at: *http://dx.doi.org/10.1787/9789264096875-en* and *www.oecd.org/environment/households/greeningbehaviour*.

The rest of the chapter is structured as follows: Section 2 examines the main factors encouraging the consumption of organic food. The role of labelling and certification is discussed in Section 3, and Section 4 reviews possible difference in attitude and behaviour towards organic food products across various types of households. The next section analyses respondents' WTP a price premium to consume organic food products. The chapter concludes with a discussion of the main policy implications.

2. Main motivations to consume organic food

The survey distinguished five categories of organic food products: fresh fruit and vegetables, milk and other dairy products, eggs, meat and poultry, and bread, pasta, rice and cereal. The percentage of households who reported actually consuming organic food was the highest in Sweden and Italy for all different food types, as well as in the Czech Republic, Korea and Mexico. Fruits and vegetables are the most popular organic item followed by eggs, while dairy products come last (see Figure 6.1). Swedes show high percentages of households consuming organic for all food categories with more than 80% reporting that they consume organic fruits and vegetables while Dutch are the least likely to consume organic.

Respondents were also asked to estimate the percentage of their household expenditure on a range of different organic items. Eggs ranked in first place overall. Australians, Italians and Swedes were found to have the highest proportion of household expenditure on the organic products in question (around 30%). For all five products, households reported that more than 20% of their total expenditure was on organic food.

Respondents were also asked to rank a list of 6 factors in order of importance in their motivation to start consuming (or to consume more) organic food products. Empirical evidence on households' main drivers to consume organic food, as well as possible obstacles to an increase in consumption levels helps guide policy makers. For instance, such information can be used to help focus the message conveyed to consumers in public information campaigns.

Figure 6.1. **Percentage of households who reported consuming organic food, by category, for selected countries**

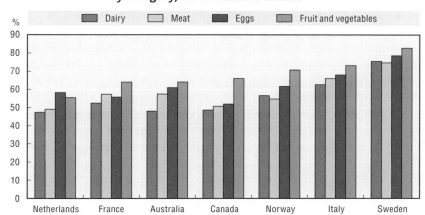

Note: The percentages have been calculated by excluding those who do not know if they consume organic or not.
Source: OECD Project on Household Behaviour and Environmental Policy.

Lower price is ranked first to consume more organic food

The responses indicate that lower price is ranked first by respondents in encouraging them to consume more organic food. Over 50% of the respondents stated prices as very important. Figure 6.2 summarises the results and shows

Figure 6.2. **Motivations to consume more organic food products**

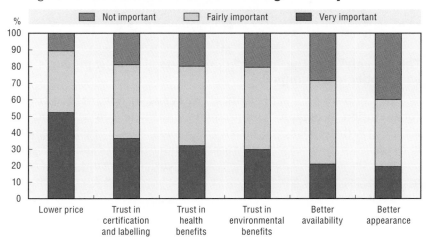

Source: OECD Project on Household Behaviour and Environmental Policy.

that trust in certification comes second (37%) followed by trust in health and in environmental benefits (around 30%), while the availability and better appearance of products seems to play a more limited role (around 20%).

However, the relative importance of the role of prices in influencing organic consumption appears to vary across countries. Figure 6.3 shows that price was most likely to be ranked as a very important factor in France (68%), and that countries least concerned with price were Norway (38%) and Korea (37%).

Figure 6.3. **The importance of price in encouraging respondents to consume more organic food, by country**

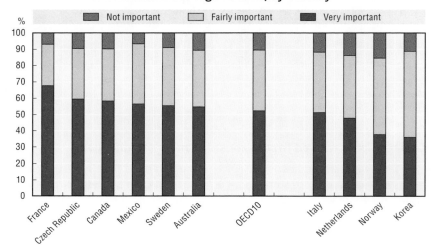

Source: OECD Project on Household Behaviour and Environmental Policy.

The "private" and the "public" dimensions of organic products both motivate consumption

Consumers can expect different types of advantages from the consumption of organic food products, and these can be distinguished according to their "public" or "private" dimension. Private benefits are reflected in factors such as the expected taste and health benefits of consuming organic products. On the other hand, the "public" dimension of organic food is reflected in factors such as the environmental benefits, impacts on animal welfare, and support for local farmers.

Overall, respondents tended to attach more importance to private benefits of organic food consumption (see Figure 6.4). However, public environmental benefits were also deemed to be important motivations. Animal welfare and support for local farmers were considered to be least important.

Figure 6.4. **Public *versus* private motivation to consume organic food, OECD10**

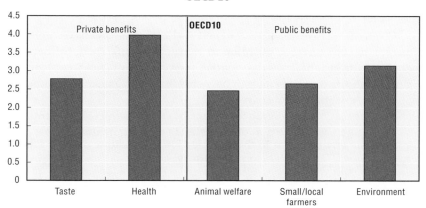

Note: The y axis represents the average rank (5 highest, 1 lowest) – this rank question was only for people who consumed organic food.

Source: OECD Project on Household Behaviour and Environmental Policy.

Differences appear when looking at results by country, as illustrated in Figure 6.5 in the case of Sweden and Korea. Respondents from Sweden generally rank the public dimensions of organic food consumption higher than private concerns, while the opposite is true in Korea. The importance of animal welfare as a factor in encouraging households to consume more

Figure 6.5. **Comparing "public" and "private" motivation to consume organic food in Sweden and Korea**

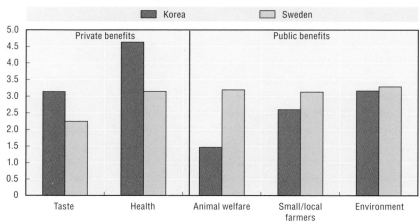

Note: The y axis represents the average rank (5 highest, 1 lowest) – this rank question was only for people who consumed organic food.

Source: OECD Project on Household Behaviour and Environmental Policy.

organic food varies significantly between countries, with the Dutch and Swedes caring the most strongly for animals and the Italians and Koreans ranking animal welfare the lowest.

Given the relative importance of personal health and public environmental concerns in consumers' motivation to consume organic food, further efforts were made to disentangle the relative importance of these two concerns. Figure 6.6 shows the percentage of households ranking personal health factors higher than environmental concerns.

Figure 6.6. **Proportion of households ranking health higher than the environment in their motivation to consume organic food, by country**

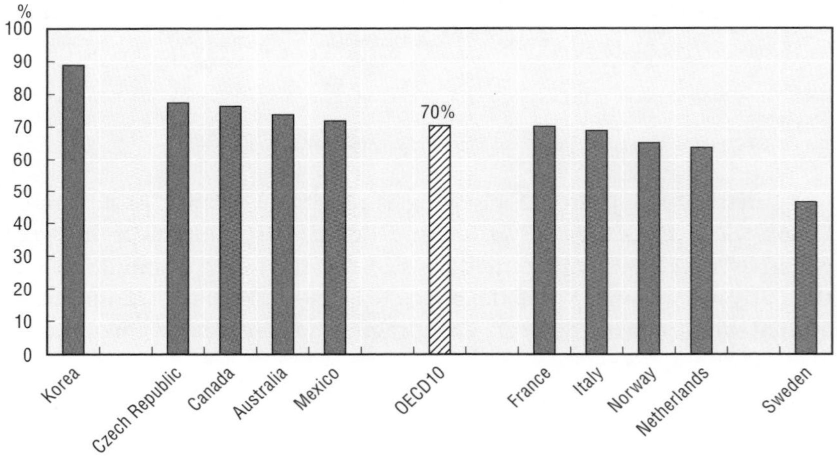

Source: OECD Project on Household Behaviour and Environmental Policy.

Seven out of ten respondents ranked the health benefits of organic food as more important than the preservation of the environment in their motivation to consume organic food. Health benefits were ranked as more important than environmental ones in all countries with the exception of Sweden. Korea had the highest preference for health with almost 90% ranking health benefits as more important than the preservation of the environment, followed by the Czech Republic, Canada, Australia and Mexico. Health concerns seem to be particularly important for "fresh fruits and vegetables" and this result is not surprising as chemical (pesticide) residues are perceived to be a particularly important health issue especially for these products.

In order to further refine the comparison on the impacts of health and environmental concerns in the individual purchase decision, respondents were asked to indicate if they would continue to consume organic products if

126

it was proved that organic food is better for personal health, but that there is no indication that it is better for the environment, or in the opposite case if organic food is better for the environment, but there is no indication that it is better for personal health. Results indicate that a greater proportion of respondents would continue to consume organic food products in the second case (52%) than in the first case (45%), confirming the importance of heath aspects in the motivation of households to consume organic food.

These results emphasise the importance of the message conveyed in information-based instruments. Both the expected public and private dimension seem to matter to a certain extent in individual motivation to consume organic products in all countries surveyed, although the relative significance of each may vary across countries. As a result, communication campaigns making reference to these two dimensions are likely to be effective, all the more so when taking into account country differences.[4] For instance, in light of the survey results, information campaigns emphasising the preservation of the environment can be expected to have a stronger impact on consumers in Sweden than in a country like Korea.

However, it should be emphasised that since clear evidence on the environmental and health benefits of organic food is sometimes lacking, information campaigns emphasising these messages need to be carefully designed by decision makers.

3. The role of labelling and certification

All 10 countries surveyed have organic labelling and the main logos used at the national level were shown to respondents. For some countries, supranational labels were also displayed in the questionnaire, like the EU organic logo used by EU member states to ensure compliance with EU organic farming regulation.

When presented with visual images of actual organic labels in the different countries, approximately half of respondents recognised the labels, but this varied widely by country as Figure 6.7 shows. Sweden had the highest level of recognition at 97%, followed by France at 87% and Norway at 75%. Mexico had the lowest level of recognition at 10%, with Canada, Italy and Australia at low, but higher levels at 18%, 25% and 29% respectively. It is interesting to note that, with the exception of Sweden which has both high levels of recognition and consumption of organic food, Mexico, Italy, Korea and the Czech Republic report high consumption of organic food, but they have low levels of organic label recognition.

Previous evidence has found that ease of identification of labels is key to steer organic food consumption, and the multiplicity of organic logos appears as an obstacle to the market take-up. The clarity of the message conveyed to consumers is moreover a priority area at the European Union level where,

Figure 6.7. **Actual organic food label recognition and use, by country**

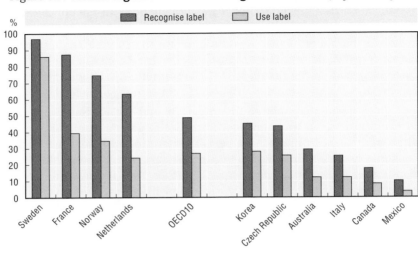

Source: OECD Project on Household Behaviour and Environmental Policy.

from July 2010, the use of the EU logo became compulsory and a new logo is to replace the current one with a view to improve recognition.[5]

However, identification of labels does not seem to be an issue in most of the countries surveyed with approximately half of the respondents finding it easy to identify organic food labels (see Figure 6.8). Canada and Sweden had the highest percentage of respondents (approximately 60%) finding it very easy or fairly easy to identify organic food labels. Koreans, Australians and Mexicans found it the most difficult to identify organic food labels with over half of the respondents finding it very difficult or fairly difficult to identify the labels.

Identification of labels is one thing, but understanding their meaning is quite another. More than half of the respondents also reported finding it easy to understand organic food labels. The percentage of respondents finding it difficult to understand was the lowest in Norway (35%) and Sweden (32%), while Koreans and Australians found it the most difficult to understand. The results show that the proportion of organic expenditure is the lowest for those who find it very difficult to understand organic food labels highlighting the importance of improving the understandability of labels.

The survey results also highlight the importance of trust in labelling and certification in encouraging more organic food consumption. Indeed, trust in certification and labelling was ranked second after price in factors encouraging respondents to consume more (or start consuming) organic food products. However, relative to price there was much more variation across countries in the importance of certification in encouraging more organic

Figure 6.8. **Ease of identification of organic food labels when buying products, by country**

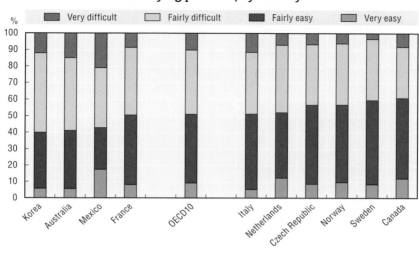

Source: OECD Project on Household Behaviour and Environmental Policy.

Figure 6.9. **Trust in certification and labelling in encouraging respondents to consume more organic food, by country**

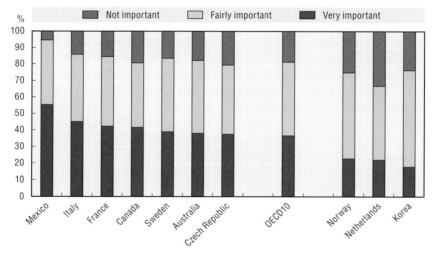

Source: OECD Project on Household Behaviour and Environmental Policy.

consumption (Figure 6.9). Mexico and Italy were the most concerned with trustworthy certification, with 55% and 45% reporting that it is very important. Norway, the Netherlands and Korea were the least concerned with 23%, 22% and 18% respectively considering it very important.

4. Main difference in attitudes and behaviour across households

Implementing tailored information and promotion campaigns to well-defined types of consumers is listed as a key action in the European Action Plan for Organic Food and Farming.[6] A number of EU countries have initiated multi-annual programmes focussing on specific target groups: households living in medium and large cities with medium and high incomes and education as well as mothers with children in the Czech Republic 2007-10 campaign; occasional users and potential light users in the Dutch 2006-08 promotion programme; and families, especially with children, in the Italian 2004-07 programme on biological products.

Who consumes organic products?

The questionnaire allows us to analyse how organic food purchasing and consumption may be influenced by individual and household characteristics such as age, education or family size. With a few exceptions, these variables do not show up as having a significant impact either on the decision to buy organic food, or on the level of consumption. This is an interesting result in itself, casting doubt on the relevance of targeting public information campaigns according to such characteristics.

Income appears to play a role in influencing the level of consumption for certain food categories only (*i.e.* food and vegetables) and does not seem to affect the decision to buy organic food, or at least not in any of the four food categories examined. However, both the probability to consume organic food and the level of organic food consumption are found to increase with income in some studies (Zhang *et al.*, 2008).

In line with previous findings in the literature, younger consumers appear as more likely to purchase organic food (Zepeda and Li, 2007; Loureiro and Lotade, 2005), with a few exceptions (Zhang *et al.*, 2008). With relatively lower income for younger consumers, this translates into relatively small increases in effective demand.

Gender does not seem to have a clear effect on organic food consumption, contrary to previous empirical work which suggested that gender has a significant effect with women more likely to purchase organic food than men and to state a higher willingness-to-pay (Rimal *et al.*, 2005). But it should be noted that results on gender are sometimes contradictory and other studies show the opposite trend (Wandel and Bugge, 1997).

Contrary to previous studies, men in multi-adult households report that they purchase more organic food than women. In any case, the survey results on gender suggest that even when gender differences are more evident in attitudes and behaviour towards environmental issues, this does not necessarily imply that these differences should be taken into account in environmental policy. However, some national public information campaigns on organic food have been recently designed to specifically target women, like the Italian promotion campaigns (2004-07).

Whether you live in a rural or an urban area seems to have no significant effect on organic food consumption. In line with the literature, findings are unclear on the effects of education contrary to recent evidence showing that consumption of organic food products increases with education (Zhang *et al.*, 2008).

In conclusion, only a few of the socio-economic and demographic variables examined are found to have a significant impact on organic food consumption. Devoting efforts toward the development of targeted information campaigns may be ineffective.

Does it make a difference if organic food is already consumed?

The survey results suggest, however, that a more relevant differentiation may instead be between those who already consume organic food products and those who do not. This result can be used by policy makers when it comes to the design of public information campaigns.

Interestingly, in the survey, the main drivers which encourage people to start consuming organic food may differ from those which encourage existing consumers to increase the relative importance of organic food in their purchases (Figure 6.10). While relative price is the most important factor in both cases, the role of availability seems to have a more important role for those who already consume at least some organic food.

This can be seen more clearly in Figure 6.11. In the case of availability, the slope of the curve is clearly the steepest when going from 0% to 1-5% of total food expenditures on organic food products, for all four food categories. This indicates that availability has a distinct role to play in encouraging people to start consuming organic food. Conversely, there is no discernible trend in the case of price.

5. Willingness-to-pay for organic foods

In the questionnaire, respondents were asked to indicate how much they would be willing to pay for a given organic food product above the price of a conventional substitute. Five food categories were distinguished: "fresh fruits and vegetables", "milk and dairy products", "eggs", "meat and poultry" and "bread, pasta, rice and cereals".[7]

The survey results are similar to the usual distribution found in the literature (Figure 6.12), where most consumers are either not willing to pay a premium for organic products or willing to pay a small price premium. Overall, almost 30% of respondents are not willing to pay any premium for organic foods. Less than 25%

Figure 6.10. **Comparing motivations to start consuming
and to consume more organic food**

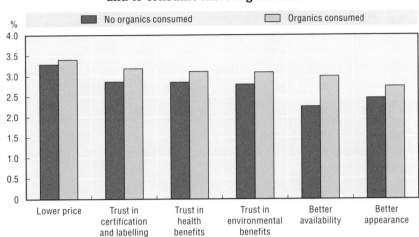

Note: The average importance of motivating factors in encouraging respondents to start or to increase organic consumption is calculated by applying a weight of 1 to responses of Not at all important, 2 to Not important, 3 to Fairly important and 4 to Very important.

Source: OECD Project on Household Behaviour and Environmental Policy.

Figure 6.11. **The importance of "better availability" and "lower price"
in the motivation to start consuming and to consume more organic food,
by groups**

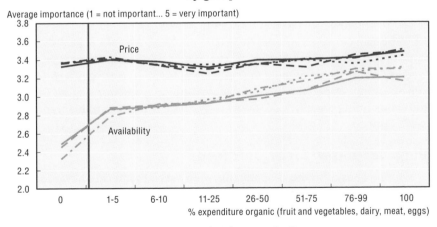

Source: OECD Project on Household Behaviour and Environmental Policy.

are willing to pay more than 5% more than for conventional foods. Just 3% of households are willing to pay a premium of more than 30%. These results indicate that the perceived benefit from the consumption of organic products is still somewhat limited.

Figure 6.12. **Willingness-to-pay (percentage price increase) for organic food, OECD10**

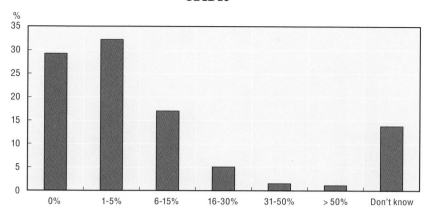

Note: These percentages have been calculated by taking the mean percentage of the 5 food groups for each willingness-to-pay category.
For example the average is taken of proportion of people for each food group stating they are not willing to pay any premium for organic food (0%) where the result 29% is the average of (28% fruit + vegetables, 29% dairy, 30% eggs, 30% cereal and 29% meat).
Source: OECD Project on Household Behaviour and Environmental Policy.

This result is consistent across product categories covered in the countries surveyed. Willingness-to-pay did not differ significanltly by food group, with only a slightly higher willingness-to-pay for organic fruits and vegetables. However, it should be noted that the actual price premium paid by consumers can be substantially higher across countries for specific food products (Turco, 2002). Examples of studies which have found particularly high price premium include eggs and poultry in the United States (Oberholtzer *et al.*, 2006) and pork in Canada (Organic Agricultural Centre of Canada, 2003).

Nevertheless, some significant variations exist across countries as indicated in Figure 6.13. The proportion of respondents that were not willng to pay any premium for organic food is the highest in the Netherlands (45%) followed by France (42%), Canada (37%), Australia (35%) and Italy (32%).

Willingness-to-pay for organic food does not appear to be clearly related to income. This is consistent with the findings of some early studies (Wilkins and Hillers, 1994; Buzby *et al.*, 1995), but contrary to the results of more recent studies which show a positive relationship between the likelihood of purchasing organic products and paying a price premium for organic food, and income levels (Torjusen *et al.*, 1999; Hill and Lynchechaun, 2002; O'Donovan and McCarthy, 2002).

Findings confirm that WTP for organic food increases with education for all products. The results also show that respondents who live in urban areas have a higher mean WTP for organic foods. In addition, attitudinal variables such as

Figure 6.13. **Percentage of respondents not willing to pay any price premium for organic food by country**

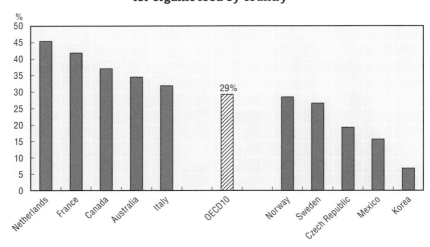

Source: OECD Project on Household Behaviour and Environmental Policy.

concern for the environment increase the WTP more for organic foods. However, consumers currently willing to pay high premiums for organic foods would like to have more confidence in the importance of these benefits. This result confirms the general finding that knowledge and awareness about organic products seem to have some significant effects on consumer attitudes and the WTP a price premium for organic food.

It is interesting to note that consumers who are not willing to pay a premium for organic foods do not trust the actual certification systems. This suggests that improvements in certification systems are key to tap the potential market for organic food products.

6. Conclusions and policy implications

The results clearly stress the impact that labelling and information campaigns may have on increasing demand for organic food. The findings of the survey provide a number of new insights to increase the impacts of such measures on consumers.

First of all, households perceive a complex mix of public and private benefits associated with the consumption of organic food products. While both private and public factors are of importance, the balance between the two is different across countries. The relative weight of different factors should be borne in mind.

Overall, perceived personal health attributes rank highest, and as such stressing health would have the greatest impact. However, it must be remembered that the epidemiological evidence concerning the health benefits is mixed.

Perceived environmental benefits are also important. Information programmes and labelling schemes which focus on such benefits would also likely have a positive impact on consumption. More generally, government measures aimed at sensitising people to relevant environmental concerns (e.g. water quality, biodiversity), would indirectly increase the demand for organic food.

The results also give some useful indication on target groups for information and promotion campaigns. Demographic and socio-economic characteristics (e.g. age, education) appear to be – with some exceptions – relatively unimportant. However, it may be more appropriate to tailor information programmes differentiating between those who already consume organic food and those who do not.

While labelling identification and understanding do not appear to be an issue in most of the countries surveyed, there are some countries where there is still work to be done. For instance, in Australia, Korea and Mexico recognition and ease of understanding of labels is relatively low, and as a consequence the use of such labels is also relatively low. Improving trust in labelling and certification appears as another important factor, and governments can have a significant role to play there. Increasing consumer trust emerges as a key factor in encouraging consumption of organic food products.

Survey findings also stress the importance of combining demand-side and supply-side policy instruments to promote organic products. Price is perceived as a major obstacle to consuming more organic products, confirming the importance of price reduction to steer consumption. Well-designed financial support schemes targeting organic food production would lower prices, but the benefits of such public expenditures need to be weighed carefully.

Lastly, the results also provide some useful insights on how governments may increase household willingness-to-pay for organic food products. While, overall, consumers are not willing to pay a high premium relative to conventional foods, government measures targeted at improving trust in certification and labelling and at raising environmental awareness would increase demand. However, this needs to be underpinned by reliable evidence on the environmental and health benefits.

Summing up the main lessons for policy makers, the survey results reassert the key role that communication campaigns and public education can play to stimulate the consumption of organic food products. The results give indications on the messages likely to have the most significant effect on the public, and on opportunities to target communication campaigns on specific types of consumers. It also underlines the complementary role of labelling and certification, and of supply-side measures targeted at price and availability.

Notes

1. This characteristic of "credence" goods distinguishes them from "experience" goods.

2. COM(2004)415 Final.

3. See *http://ec.europa.eu/agriculture/organic/eu-policy/promotion-programmes_en*.

4. See *http://ec.europa.eu/agriculture/organic/toolbox/messages-slogans_en*.

5. Council Regulation (EC) No. 834/2007 of 28 June 2007 on organic production and labelling of organic product.

6. COM(2004)415 Final.

7. The Contingent Valuation method was used in the survey to elicit the willingness-to-pay (WTP) where respondents face a hypothetical purchasing situation in which they have to indicate the premium they are willing to pay for a given product, expressed as a percentage above the reference price, the price of conventional products (Haneman, 1984). Respondents were asked to choose among six classes of WTP: 0%, 1-5%, 6-15%, 16-30%, 31-50%, > 50%. The use of contingent valuation method to elicit willingness-to-pay (WTP) for food quality attributes is quite common in the literature.

References

Buzby *et al.* (1995), "Valuing Food Safety and Nutrition", *Using Contingent Valuation to Value Food Safety: A Case Study of Grapefruit and Pesticide Residues.*

Hill, H. and F. Lynchehaun (2002), "Organic Milk: Attitudes and Consumption Patterns", *British Food Journal*, Vol. 104(7), pp. 526-542.

IFOAM (2007), *The World of Organic Agriculture: Statistics and Emerging Trends 2007*, Federation of Organic Agriculture Movements, Switzerland.

Loureiro, M.L. and J. Lotade (2005), "Do Fair Trade and Eco-labels in Coffee Wake Up the Consumer Conscience?", *Ecological Economics*, Vol. 53(1), pp. 129-138.

Oberholtzer, L., C. Greene and E. Lopez (2006), "Organic Poultry and Eggs Capture High Price Premiums and Growing Share of Specialty Markets", *Outlook Report from the Economic Research Service*, LDP-M-150-01, USDA.

O'Donovan, P. and M. McCarthy (2002), "Irish Consumer Preference for Organic Meat", *British Food Journal*, Vol. 104(3/4/5), pp. 353-370.

OECD (2008a), *Environmental Outlook to 2030*, OECD, Paris.

Rimal, A.P., W. Moon and S. Balasubramanian (2005), "Agro-biotechnology and Organic Food Purchase in the United Kingdom", *British Food Journal*, Vol. 107(2), pp. 84-97.

Torjusen, N. and M. Wandel (1999), "Organic Food: Consumers' Perceptions and Dietary Choices", *SIFO-Report*, No. 5-1999.

Turco, G. (2002), "Organic Food – An Opportunity, at Who's Expense?", *Industry Note*, Food and Agribusiness Research, Rabobank International, Sydney.

Wandel, M. and A. Bugge (1997), "Environmental Concerns in Consumer Evaluation of Food Quality", *Food Quality and Preferences*, Vol. 8(1), pp. 19-26.

Wilkins, J.L. and V.N. Hillers (1994), "Influences of Pesticide Residue and Environmental Concerns on Organic Food Preference among Food Cooperative Members and Non-members in Washington State", *Journal of Nutrition Education*, Vol. 26(1), pp. 26-33.

Zepeda, L. and Jinghan Li (2007), "Characteristics of Organic Food Shoppers", *Journal of Agricultural and Applied Economics*, Vol. 39(1), pp. 17-28.

Zhang, F., C.L. Huang, B.H. Lin and J.E. Epperson (2008), "Modeling Fresh Organic Produce Consumption with Scanner Data: A Generalised Double Hurdle Model Approach", *Agribusiness*, Vol. 24(4), pp. 510-522.

Chapter 7

Conclusions and Policy Implications

This concluding chapter presents important general cross-cutting policy lessons emerging from this survey on the design of demand-side measures and how to increase their impact at the individual or household level. It also summarises the main findings in the five areas examined: water use, energy use, personal transport choices, organic food consumption, and waste generation and recycling. The chapter draws policy implications on how to best choose and combine instruments to improve the effectiveness and efficiency of policies targeting the greening of household behaviour. It also shows the way forward with the implementation of a new round of the survey in 2011.

1. Introduction

Environmental pressures from households are significant, and their impacts are projected to increase in the future (OECD, 2008a). The aim of the OECD activity on Environmental Policy and Household Behaviour is to better understand factors driving households' environment-related decisions in order to inform policy design and implementation. Five areas of particular concern to decision makers, given their environmental significance, have been examined: residential energy use, domestic water consumption, waste generation and recycling, organic food consumption, and personal transport choices.

Drawing upon data collected in an OECD Household Survey, the factors that affect households' decision making in these five areas have been analysed. The results presented in this publication are based upon the analysis of more than 10 000 responses collected in 2008 in ten countries: Australia, Canada, the Czech Republic, France, Italy, Korea, Mexico, the Netherlands, Norway and Sweden.

This work also provides insight on the impacts of changes in household structure, characteristics and lifestyles, on consumption patterns and resulting pressures on the environment in the future. This is important for the anticipation of long-term trends in the areas of energy, food, transport, water and waste.

This concluding chapter presents general cross-cutting policy lessons emerging from this survey and the main area-specific findings and policy implications to best craft policies targeting household consumption patterns. It also shows the way forward with the implementation of a new round of the survey in 2011 as a follow-up OECD contribution on how to best spur behavioural change with environmental policy.

2. General cross-cutting policy lessons

Important general policy lessons emerge from this work on the design of demand-side measures and how to increase their impact at the individual or household level. Key areas where survey findings inform policy design include the choice and combination of instruments as well as measures targeting different consumer groups. This work brings to the fore additional considerations for the design of policies pursuing behavioural change.

Providing the right incentives is key

First, the role played by incentive-based instruments to spur behavioural change is clearly confirmed. The survey shows that metering and billing encourage energy and water savings. Households charged for the water they use are also more likely to install water-efficient equipment at home and consume approximately 20% less water. In addition, waste charges increase recycling volumes and affect waste prevention behaviour. Finally, fuel costs are found to have a negative effect on car use, confirming the existing literature. This suggests that changing relative prices (for electricity, water, fuel) is necessary if emissions are to be reduced and natural resources to be conserved.

While measures that have a direct effect on prices such as charges or taxes appear to be necessary, they do not prove to always be sufficient, particularly for pressing environmental concerns. The impacts of economic incentives may, for instance, be limited in the short term, but increase with time. Evidence based on panel data in the areas of transport, energy or water underlines the existence of this time-lag. Consumers need time to adjust their holdings of durable equipment and invest in energy-efficient or water-efficient appliances. In a similar way, the response to the introduction of fuel-related taxes is limited in the first instance to reducing the use of motor vehicles while, in the medium term, households can change vehicles, or even travel mode. In the longer term, the choice of location of residence may be adjusted to increase the proximity to public transportation.

Even if pricing policies are considered as effective and efficient, they can raise distributional concerns. The survey provides new evidence that low-income households are the most adversely affected by increases in water charges. The political acceptability of environment-related taxes or charges can be improved by the use of information tools to communicate how they can contribute to a better environment. Moreover, the distributional impacts of other measures (such as standards) may be just as significant, although less transparent (OECD, 2006). In addition, distributional impacts may be alleviated through the reduction of other taxes or the provision of direct financial support to low-income households (such as child allowance).

Information and awareness play a significant complementary role

In addition to the significant role played by incentive-based instruments, the survey findings indicate that "softer" instruments, based on the provision of information to consumers, and education can have a substantial complementary role to induce changes on the demand side; a more substantial role than what earlier assessments of policy instruments generally find.

Environmental awareness

An important policy-relevant message is that being concerned with the environment has a clear influence on a number of decisions. The role of attitudinal factors is consistent across the areas examined. For example, environmental awareness is a main driver for water-saving behaviours and reduces the likelihood of owning a car. Concern for the environment also influences demand for energy-efficient appliances and renewable energy, as well as the intensity of waste recycling and decisions to consume organic food.

This indicates that an important task for governments may be to multiply information campaigns in order to raise people's environmental awareness. This may, of course, spur behavioural change. In addition, increased awareness of the environmental impacts of consumption choices may increase the political acceptability of policies, facilitating their implementation. Once in place, enforcement costs may also be reduced since the policies are more likely to be seen as justified by households.

The survey also clearly indicates, in all five areas covered, that the level of *educational attainment* increases pro-environmental values, attitudes and behaviours. This important finding suggests that governments have a significant role to play to promote "greener" behaviour by increasing the general level of educational attainment, as well as through targeted public information campaigns.

Information on characteristics and consumption of products

The survey also stresses the usefulness of providing information on products' characteristics to consumers so that they can make informed decisions. Results suggest that *eco-labels* need to be clear and comprehensible and, as such, measures that encourage ease of identification and understanding of eco-labels are likely to be more effective. Moreover, labels prove to be particularly effective if they relate to both the public and private benefits of the good or service. An example is the reduced energy bill resulting from energy-saving behaviour that also leads to a reduction in greenhouse gas emissions.

The possible personal health benefits associated with organic agriculture is another example. Eco-labels could exploit the potential for private benefits to a larger extent since people's willingness-to-pay for public benefits, such as improved environmental quality, is often limited. Understanding the relative importance of *"public" and "private" motivations* is of value for policy design, particularly for measures providing information (labels, information campaigns), allowing consumers to make informed choices.

Another related policy-relevant finding is that information on the level of consumption can, by itself, be a valuable tool to change behaviour. Results stress the observed *lack of knowledge* among respondents about their actual water and electricity consumption. This suggests that recent campaigns to provide improved information to consumers, by installing smart meters that display accurate real-time information on energy use in the home, are likely to affect households' behaviour, even if there is no change in relative prices.

The importance of norms

In addition, this empirical work emphasises the role of *norms*, particularly in households' motivation to recycle material or not. Policies have an effect on people's intrinsic and social norms – how they see the environmental good which is to be protected. Policy makers need to take into account the effect of different policy measures on norms. For instance, some measures may result in reduced voluntary provision of the good in question. This also suggests that information policy and training programmes to help make informed decisions can play a role in stimulating personal motives by stressing the social aspects of environment-friendly behaviours such as recycling and waste prevention. Further work on the origin of norms and how they interact with decisions could be usefully carried out.

Operating both the supply and the demand sides

This work stresses the importance of operating both the demand and the supply sides. The demand by households for environmental quality is important. But the supply of environment-related services to households also clearly matters as it increases the range of substitution possibilities. Governments have a significant role to play in this latter case.

The results indicate that in a number of areas (transport, recycling, energy) the provision of adequate *infrastructure* and services can have an impact at least as important, if not more important than relative prices. Moreover, environmental policy measures tend to have a more significant effect on individual behaviour when implemented in combination with investments in related environmental services. The survey confirms that access to public transport affects car ownership and car use. Installing meters also encourages people to reduce energy and water consumption, through both behavioural change and investment in more efficient appliances. Furthermore, the presence and quality of collection services for recyclables is found to increase recycling participation and intensity, and recycling levels are highest when households have access to door-to-door collection services.

However, it is particularly important to bear in mind the administrative costs associated with the provision of infrastructures. In the area of waste, for instance, while a drop-off scheme may be less effective in terms of increasing recycling rates than a door-to-door collection scheme, the latter is likely to be much more costly in terms of service provision.

Given the importance of economies of scale involved in the provision of recyclable waste collection schemes, public transportation or electricity supply, the tendency is for a single firm to dominate the market. Since so many sectors that are environment-intensive are also natural monopolies, this implies that environmental considerations need to be carefully scrutinised by the regulator.

In addition, the findings point to the fact that some environment-friendly decisions tend to be only weakly driven by demand and thus may rely heavily upon complementary measures targeting the supply side. The survey indicates that, in line with the results of other studies, households do not appear to be ready to pay much to use "green" energy. This implies that if governments wish to source a share of electricity from renewables, measures on the demand side will have to be complemented by supply-side measures (feed-in tariffs, renewable energy certificates). In a similar way, households generally have a low willingness-to-pay for recycling services. Finally, households are not willing to pay for organic products, generally less than 15% more than for conventional products.* This result implies that household demand is unlikely to be enough to secure an uptake of some markets and that supply-side measures targeted on price and availability have a significant complementary role to play.

Using a mix of instruments

This work confirms that using a mix of instruments is likely to increase the impact of environmental policies targeting behavioural change in some cases. The survey results provide useful insight to policy makers on how best to combine instruments in order to increase the efficiency and effectiveness of policies (see also OECD, 2007).

First, when implementing policy packages targeting household behavioural change, it is central to keep in mind that there may be a significant *time-lag* for households to adjust. Taking into account this lag in the responsiveness to price incentives is particularly important when addressing certain environmental concerns (such as water scarcity). The time horizon involved in decision-making processes can vary significantly across policy areas. Short-term responses may be smaller when households are adjusting their stock of durables, investing in energy – or water – efficient equipment for instance, and reduction in energy or water consumption may be limited during this period. This underlines how instruments can usefully complement each other. The impact of pricing can be more significant in the long term but well-designed information-based measures can make a difference in the short term as the survey results suggest.

---

* Previous studies usually find a higher price premium for organic food products compared to conventional ones (see Oberholtzer *et al.*, 2006).

Another interesting finding emerging from the survey, which also points to the *complementary* role of instruments, is that some factors can have a greater impact on discrete decisions such as costly investments (whether or not to buy an energy-efficient appliance or invest in thermal insulation), while others will have a larger impact on everyday decisions (whether to turn off the stand-by mode or reduce indoor temperature). For instance, environmental awareness appears to reduce the likelihood of owning a car, but has little impact on car use once you own one. Being aware of such differences can be valuable for policy makers, helping them to ensure that policies are complementary and reflect the factors that households take into account for different decisions. For instance, the provision of well-designed information tools allowing customers to make informed choices at the point of purchase, such as labels on vehicle CO_2 emissions, can be usefully combined with fuel taxes, which may have a stronger impact on intensity of use.

However, while the survey reflects clear complementarities between instruments, some forms of *redundancy* emerge too. Taking the area of waste, there is some evidence that unit pricing and recyclable waste collection systems are substitutes rather than complements from the perspective of their impact on recycling levels. However, it must be emphasised that unit waste fees provide incentives for any strategy to avoid putting out waste for disposal, including prevention, while collection or drop-off services for recyclable waste only favour recycling.

The results also underline the existence of possible *conflicting effects* when applying a package of measures to target a similar externality. For instance, the adoption of economic incentives may have adverse effects when information tools are geared towards households' non-monetary motivations for environmental behaviour, such as personal and social norms. In the case of recycling, intrinsic motivations, such as a sense of civic duty, appear to play a significant role in explaining recycling efforts. Therefore, the adoption of a pricing system, or making recycling mandatory rather than voluntary may erode behaviour based on moral motivations. Policy makers need to be wary of that in order to avoid "crowding out" effects.

In addition, the survey suggests that in the policy mix used to spur behavioural change, *targeting measures* can be relevant in some cases. The results show significant variation in environmental behaviour and responsiveness to policy measures across households' demographic and socio-economic characteristics. In most cases, this variation just reflects different preferences, and is not necessarily policy-relevant. In other cases, it can be pertinent for policy makers to tailor measures for different groups, for instance when market barriers and failures particularly affect some households, such as tenants (split incentives) or low-income households (credit market failures). However, whatever the criteria used, the administrative cost associated with the targeting

145

of policies must be borne in mind when assessing the efficiency of a given policy as the benefits may not be sufficient to justify the additional cost, which may be considerable.

The survey gives some useful indication with respect to the identification of specific groups for which information and promotion campaigns would be most effective. Demographic and socio-economic characteristics (age, education) can be used to define distinct segments of the population according to their impact on the environment (for example, differences in motivations). For instance, information campaigns to modify personal transport choices will be most effective if they target those groups which have higher car use: men, the middle-aged, and those with higher incomes and education. Survey results also suggest that policies may be usefully targeted according to other characteristics. For instance, targeting measures according to whether households live in rural or urban areas may result in increased recycling levels as well as according to housing type, and focusing measures on detached or semi-detached houses *versus* apartments can matter for waste disposal schemes.

Finally, this work underlines the significant complementary role that *non-environmental policies* can play, such as revenue redistribution measures addressing distributional issues or housing policy. Many environmental policies are likely to have adverse distributional effects and the survey provides evidence on the adverse effect of some measures, particularly in the area of water consumption. Low-income households are likely to be most affected by increases in water charges as they spend on residential water of their income more than twice the proportion relative to high-income households. When introducing measures to address possible disparities between income groups, policy makers need to ensure that the economic efficiency and environmental effectiveness of the policy remains intact. In terms of efficiency, it will usually be preferable to address distributional impacts outside the context of the environmental policy design itself, in order to retain the incentive to improve the environmental problem (OECD, 2006).

The survey confirms that some household groups may be less likely to adopt a particular environmental behaviour because their status on the property market gives them different incentives, and that targeted measures may be usefully applied. *Landlords* will have few incentives to invest in energy-efficient equipment if they rent their property (house or flat) as such investments will mainly benefit the tenant (lower energy bill). On the other hand, *tenants* will have few incentives to invest in a property they do not own, especially if they are not planning to occupy it for a long period of time. The same market failure discourages landlords from investing in water-efficient equipment or water conservation devices. To address this issue of split incentives, targeted housing policy measures may therefore be introduced to complement environmental policy such as the provision of a financial incentive to landlords to make their rental properties "greener".

3. Area-specific conclusions and policy implications

Policies targeting water consumption and water quality

First and foremost, the results highlight the effectiveness of charging households for the amount of water they use as a means to promote water conservation. This action alone would, on average, lower households' water consumption by about 20%. In addition, a volumetric charge for water is found to increase the likelihood that households will adopt several water-saving behaviours and investments.

However, respondents' awareness of water consumption appears to be relatively low. As such, metering for water consumption may improve awareness of consumption and increase the marginal cost of consumption. Awareness alone seems to have an impact on investing in water-efficient appliances and adopting water-saving behaviours. This suggests that water charges can work in tandem with water-saving campaigns to reinforce water conservation. The positive and significant effect of labels on the probability of investing in water-efficient appliances underscores this point.

The manner in which incentives and policies interact may differ across segments of the population. For instance, the effects of water charging, water labelling and ownership status on investment in water-efficient equipment are comparable in size. However, there are of course significant interactions between these three factors. For instance, the value of water charging and eco-labelling are likely to be very different depending upon ownership status. While stated concern for the environment has a significant effect on most water-saving behaviours and equipment investments, the effects of environmental norms do not appear to be a significant determinant of water consumption levels.

The results also indicate that increases in the average price of water will put a greater burden on low-income households since they spend a much higher proportion of their income on their water bill than high-income households do. This is a significant policy concern, but one which is relatively easily addressed. However, it is important to keep marginal incentives intact. Full-cost water pricing, coupled with assistance to low-income households in the form of a low or zero fixed fee, or through transfer payments, will help ensure water is used efficiently and allocated equitably across residential consumers.

Concern about water quality varies by country, with concerns about health more frequently cited than taste. There are three means to address such concerns: public investment in treatment systems; private investment in purification at the tap; and drinking bottled water. The economic and environmental impacts of these three strategies are very different, and thus it is important to understand what is motivating household preferences and choices.

It is found that willingness-to-pay for improved public water treatment is relatively low, generally less than 10% of water bills. Stated willingness-to-pay is affected by income, education, gender and other factors. However, it is also affected significantly by the degree of trust in government authorities. In the absence of such trust, households will buy bottled water and in-house purification systems to secure the desired level of quality with different economic and environmental implications. In policy terms, it is interesting that concern for solid waste has a negative effect on bottled water consumption. This underscores the need to examine environmental issues in an integrated manner, and to design policies accordingly.

Policies targeting residential energy use

Several conclusions emerge from this survey on the determinants of household residential energy use. First of all, the survey clearly confirms the significant role played by electricity metering and billing to encourage energy savings at home. Results show that respondents paying charges are more likely to adopt energy-saving behaviours like turning off lights when not needed, or investing in efficiency-rated appliances and thermal insulation.

People's attitude towards the environment appears to influence energy demand. The survey shows that environmental concern, awareness and attitudes have a positive effect on energy-saving behaviour at home, as well as investments in energy-efficient equipment. Being concerned with the environment and being a member of an environmental organisation are also associated with greater demand for renewable energy. This result emphasises the complementary role that the provision of information to consumers and education can play in promoting residential energy behaviour with less impact on the environment.

The survey results underline the usefulness of targeting some measures on specific household groups with different incentives to make environment-friendly energy investments. Indeed, the findings reveal that homeowners are more likely than tenants to invest in energy-saving equipment such as thermal insulation or efficient boilers, as well as renewable energy technologies. Thus, policies where landlords are given incentives to "green" their rented properties and their tenants are given the right to recover the costs for such investments from landlords could be considered, while taking into account the administrative cost associated with targeting measures.

Finally, the results suggest that the substantial support given to renewable energy in many countries contrasts with the fairly weak voluntary demand for "green" electricity reported in this survey. While there is significant variation across countries, the survey shows that respondents are not willing to pay a significant premium to use "green" energy rather than "normal" electricity. This is in line with other studies. Indeed, relatively few households are prepared to pay more than 5% above their current electricity bill to use green energy, and almost half of them are not willing to pay anything. This finding implies that the increased use of green energy at home in the future is likely to be only weakly demand-driven and that if market penetration is to increase it is through supply-side measures.

Policies targeting waste generation and recycling

Importantly, the results indicate that charging per unit of waste generated in volume terms has a significant impact on reducing waste generation and a more limited one on recycling. Moreover, it has little effect on the decision to recycle or not, but does influence recycling levels for those who already recycle. The results indicate that the type of recyclable waste collection services provided to households has a significant effect on recycling rates. Recycling activities by households are highest for those with door-to-door collection compared to drop-off containers.

The survey shows that household waste generation is significantly affected by gender, age, education, household size and location of residence. As such, changes in household living patterns and demographic characteristics will have an impact on waste generation. For instance, continued falls in average household size will result in increased waste per capita and additional pressure on the environment. These factors have implications for policy planning.

In addition, stated concern for the environment has a positive impact on recycling. Social motivations which are distinct from explicitly environmental concerns also have an influence on recycling rates. Such intrinsic and social motivations should be taken into account in policy design and information-based campaigns.

Policies targeting personal transport choices

It is clear that demographic (age, gender, household composition), economic (income, employment status), and structural (location of residence) factors affect personal transport choices. These factors can be considered exogenous and thus not subject to direct influence through environmental policy. However, an understanding of their role is important in assessing the likely impacts of different policies on personal transport choices. Moreover, in the longer term, some of these factors – for example location of residence in relation to destination for different travel purposes – are subject to policy influence. Efforts to discourage out-of-town shopping and urban sprawl can be seen in this light, and the results of this study indicate that they will reduce car use significantly.

The results confirm the influence of the relative price of different modes on personal transport choice. While prices matter, they may not be sufficient. In order to discourage people from using their car, it is important to provide adequate infrastructure. The results clearly indicate that improving the accessibility of public transport will reduce car ownership and use, and encourage the use of public transport. However, "accessibility" needs to be carefully defined – above 15 minutes there is no discernible impact, and below five minutes the impact on car use is considerably greater.

More generally, the quality of public transport services is likely to decrease car use and increase public transport use. While rapidity and convenience are cited as being important in all countries, the other factors which also matter, personal security or improved reliability, differ by country. This is instructive for policy design – the factors which will encourage people to use public transport vary by country. In addition, a better cycling infrastructure is also likely to reduce car use, particularly in those countries where this mode is limited at present. However, the extent of variation across countries is instructive, and indicates that significant substitution can be encouraged in some countries.

Over and above the effects of factors such as price and infrastructure, it is clear that the attitude of respondents towards environmental issues has an effect on personal transport decisions. It is revealing that this effect is stronger with respect to car ownership than car use. The effect of environmental "norms" also varies by travel purpose. Norms affect travel for commuting and educational purposes. These results indicate that in some areas at least a "soft" policy would have a positive impact on substituting a car for an alternative mode.

Overall, the results underline the importance of looking at mode choice and travel purpose together. In addition, it can be concluded that a mix of push-pull instruments is required in order to encourage transport choices which are less environmentally damaging. Increasing the cost of driving and accessibility to public transport must go hand in hand. Furthermore, a combination of "hard" policies (taxes and regulations) and "soft" policies (information) is required to induce mode switching.

Policies targeting organic food consumption

The results on organic food consumption confirm the key role that communication campaigns and public education can play. Labelling and information campaigns do have an impact on demand for organic food. However, a better understanding of the balance between environment and health motivations in the decision to consume organic provides insights to how governments can increase the impacts of these measures. Overall, perceived personal health benefits rank highest and so stressing health would have the greatest impact on household decision. However, it must be remembered that the epidemiological evidence concerning the health benefits of organic foods is mixed. Perceived environmental benefits are found to be of lesser importance, nonetheless suggesting that information programmes and labelling schemes focusing on such benefits would also likely have a positive impact on organic consumption. More generally, government measures aimed at sensitising people to relevant environmental concerns (water quality, biodiversity) could increase the demand for organic food.

The survey also gives some useful indication on target groups for information and promotion campaigns. Demographic and socio-economic characteristics generally play a limited role in the motivation to consume organic foods. However, the factors which affect the level of consumption for those who already consume at least some organic food appear to differ from the factors that determine whether any organic food is consumed at all. This has implications for the targeting of campaigns and the key message to convey, with segmentation between the two groups.

Identification and understanding of labels do not appear to be an issue in most of the countries surveyed. However, improving people's trust in labelling and certification appears as an important factor, and governments can have a significant role to play there. Increasing consumers' trust emerges as a key factor in encouraging increased consumption of organic food products.

In addition, the survey findings stress the importance of policy instruments targeted on both the demand and supply sides to promote organic products. High prices relative to conventional substitutes are stated to be a major obstacle to consuming more organic products. When designing policies, this suggests a complementarity between labelling and certification and supply-side measures, including a reduction of subsidies for conventional agriculture.

Lastly, the results provide some useful insights on how governments may increase households' willingness-to-pay for organic food products. While, overall, consumers are not willing to pay a high premium relative to conventional foods, government measures targeted on improving trust in certification and labelling and on raising environmental awareness would increase demand. However, this needs to be underpinned by reliable evidence on the environmental and health benefits.

4. Moving forward

Analysis of environmental policy from the demand side is receiving increasing attention from governments, with issues such as the adoption of eco-innovations by households. A second OECD household survey will be carried out in 2010-11 with the objective of identifying changes in people's attitudes and behaviour towards the environment, as well as analysing new issues. The new survey will examine ways to promote green growth and the development of a low-carbon economy from the household perspective.

It is expected that the core of the 2008 questionnaire will be repeated with appropriate modifications where necessary in the five key areas of environmental policy (energy, food, transport, waste and water). In this way changes in consumption patterns and behaviour over time can be tracked. The new survey questionnaire will be developed by the Secretariat of the OECD Environment Directorate, with inputs from the Advisory Committee, the research teams involved in the project, other OECD directorates working in related areas and the International Energy Agency. Its design will be improved by building on the lessons learned from carrying out the first survey.

The work on Environmental Policy and Individual Change (EPIC) will contribute to key horizontal OECD work in support of international discussions and commitments. This will provide inputs to the innovation strategy and will contribute to the development of the OECD's *Green Growth Strategy*. It will also inform work on barriers to policy implementation and on subjective well-being. In addition, cross-fertilisation will be sought with the OECD PISA Survey on Educational Attainment which will include questions on the environment in its next round.

References

Oberholtzer, L., C. Greene and E. Lopez (2006), "Organic Poultry and Eggs Capture High Price Premiums and Growing Share of Specialty Markets", *Outlook Report from the Economic Research Service*, LDP-M-150-01, USDA.

OECD (2006), *The Distributional Effects of Environmental Policy*, Serret, Y. and N. Johnstone (eds.), OECD, Paris/Edward Elgar, Cheltenham, UK.

OECD (2007), *Instrument Mixes for Environmental Policy*, OECD, Paris.

OECD (2008a), *Environmental Outlook to 2030*, OECD, Paris.

ANNEX A

Methodology and Project Implementation

Survey implementation

The OECD household survey was implemented using the internet, a cost-effective and promising approach to large-scale data collection.[1] A survey provider (*Lightspeed Research*) was identified to collect responses to the questionnaire using its on-line consumer panels in different countries. The OECD chose the survey provider with care in order to minimise problems that can be associated with online surveys, such as biased samples, professional respondents and superficial responses. Thus, the survey provider's panel size, recruitment, management and representiveness were scrutinised. In particular, the rules applied to manage the panel – such as the incentive mode used for the respondent and the maximum number of surveys a panellist can respond to per year – have been carefully examined.[2]

Lightspeed Research recruits respondents through hundreds of websites in each country and uses broad-reach portals with niche websites to reach rarer demographic targets. Potential panel members are contacted through newsletters and online advertising campaigns with partner sites. Once recruited, chosen panel members are contacted by email and invited to respond to selected surveys. Panel members are given rewards for taking part in surveys. In order to ensure representativity, the sample has been stratified in each country according to different characteristics of the population (*e.g.* age, gender, region, socio-economic status). An algorithm is used to select respondents based on these variables, as well as the panel management rules (for example taking into account the maximum number of surveys a panellist can respond to each year).

Design of the questionnaire

The survey questionnaire has been developed by the Secretariat of the OECD Environment Directorate, with inputs from the Advisory Committee composed of government representatives, research teams involved in the project, other OECD Directorates working in related areas (*e.g.* Trade and

Agriculture Directorate, Committee on Consumer Policy) and the International Energy Agency. The draft questionnaire was pre-tested in Canada, Italy, Korea, Sweden and the United Kingdom in Spring 2007. The questionnaire was revised in light of the lessons learned.

The final survey instrument was implemented simultaneously in all ten countries in January-February 2008. The survey questionnaire is composed of seven parts: two parts dealing with socio-demographic and attitudinal characteristics, and five parts relating to household behaviour in the five environmental areas of interest: waste generation and recycling, personal transport choices, residential energy use, organic food consumption and water use. Mean response time for completion of the questionnaire was just over 30 minutes. The full survey questionnaire is provided in Annex A (Canadian English version).

Sample

To ensure a representative sample and avoid sample bias, the sample was stratified by income, age, gender and region in each of the ten countries (see Table A.1). For the income variable, a different approach was adopted for each country due to differences in data collection practice and availability. The data were stratified by either two or three classes based on either household or personal income, and on gross or income net of taxes. However, within the questionnaire, respondents were requested to indicate household after-tax income which allows for a consistent treatment of the data. The stratification was adjusted based upon the distribution of responses to this question in a pilot study.

Age was stratified using the following groups: 18-24, 25-34, 35-44, 45-54 and 55 years and over. Gender was approximately half male and half female, with slightly more females in all countries. Region was stratified by as few as five regions in the Netherlands and over 20 for Italy and France. The survey allowed for the collection of a unique dataset of more than 10 000 households in ten countries. Table A.1 provides a summary of the sample by country, age and gender.

Table A.1. **Summary of the sample by country, age and gender**

	Male	Female	Total		Male	Female	Total
Canada				**Czech Republic**			
18-24	71	59	130	18-24	43	76	119
25-34	79	115	194	25-34	80	84	164
35-44	99	127	226	35-44	59	64	123
45-55	79	97	176	45-55	104	96	200
55+	161	116	277	55+	58	37	95
Total	**489**	**514**	**1 003**	**Total**	**344**	**357**	**701**
Netherlands				**Sweden**			
18-24	21	74	95	18-24	34	91	125
25-34	68	107	175	25-34	85	124	209
35-44	103	120	223	35-44	99	137	236
45-55	106	89	195	45-55	105	97	202
55+	179	148	327	55+	120	114	234
Total	**477**	**538**	**1 015**	**Total**	**443**	**563**	**1 006**
France				**Norway**			
18-24	28	83	111	18-24	40	75	115
25-34	58	131	189	25-34	95	90	185
35-44	96	115	211	35-44	100	139	239
45-55	74	132	206	45-55	126	87	213
55+	278	80	358	55+	170	97	267
Total	**534**	**541**	**1 075**	**Total**	**531**	**488**	**1 019**
Mexico				**Australia**			
18-24	100	147	247	18-24	29	61	90
25-34	144	143	287	25-34	63	124	187
35-44	107	112	219	35-44	77	152	229
45-55	124	71	195	45-55	95	111	206
55+	42	19	61	55+	186	108	294
Total	**517**	**492**	**1 009**	**Total**	**450**	**556**	**1 006**
Italy				**Korea**			
18-24	65	123	279	18-24	72	111	183
25-34	153	126	273	25-34	139	121	260
35-44	149	124	227	35-44	116	118	234
45-55	117	110	450	45-55	76	84	160
55+	200	250	1 417	55+	92	71	163
Total	**684**	**733**	**188**	**Total**	**495**	**505**	**1 000**

Source: OECD Project on Household Behaviour and Environmental Policy.

Notes

1. Such a methodology has been used previously in environmental economics, particularly for contingent valuation studies. See Lindhjem and Navrud (2008), Thurston (2006), Olsen (2007), Dickie *et al.* (2007), and Berrens *et al.* (2004).

2. See *www.oecd.org/dataoecd/55/19/44101274.pdf*.

ANNEX B

OECD Questionnaire

OECD survey on household environmental behaviour 2008 questionnaire

Canadian edit master – English version

1. How would you define your status in your current primary residence?

1. Married or living as a couple.

2. Living with parents or other relatives.

3. Living alone.

4. Living as a single parent.

5. Sharing a house/flat with non-family members.

2. Thinking about purchasing responsibilities for the household (utility bills, grocery shopping, etc.), would you say that:

1. You have primary responsibility for these decisions.

2. You share responsibilities for these decisions.

3. You have no responsibility for these decisions > **close survey**.

PART A – SOCIO-DEMOGRAPHIC CHARACTERISTICS

3. Are you:

    1. Male.

    2. Female.

4. What year were you born?

5. How many adults of 18 years old or more (including yourself) live in your household?

    1. 1

    2. 2

    3. 3

    4. 4

    5. 5+

6a. How many children, under 18, live in your household?

    1. 0

    2. 1

    3. 2

    4. 3

    5. 4

    6. 5+

6b. How many of these children are under 5 years old?

    1. 0

    2. 1

    3. 2

    4. 3

    5. 4

    6. 5+

7. Which of the following regions do you currently live in?

    1.   Alberta.

    2.   British Columbia.

    3.   Manitoba.

    4.   New Brunswick.

5. Newfoundland.

6. Nova Scotia

7. Ontario.

8. Prince Edward Island.

9. Quebec.

10. Saskatchewan.

8. What is the highest level of education that you have completed?

1. Did not graduate from High School.

2. High School Graduate.

3. Some Post-Secondary Education.

4. Bachelor's Degree (BA).

5. Post Graduate Degree (Master or PhD).

6. Prefer not to answer.

9. What is your current employment status?

1. Employed full time.

2. Employed part time/casual.

3. Retired.

4. Homemaker – househusband/wife.

5. Seeking a job/unemployed.

6. In employment but not currently working (*e.g.* sick leave, maternity/paternity).

7. Student.

8. Volunteer work only.

9. Other.

10. How would you characterise your current occupation (or previous occupation if retired)?

Please select the classification which most closely characterises your occupation:

1. Liberal profession (*e.g.* medical doctor, lawyer) and teachers.

2. Middle/senior executive.

3. Self-employed in commerce, industry or agriculture.

4. Salaried employee (office).

5. Manual worker (manufacturing, agriculture, etc.).

6. Other, please specify:

11. Which of these ranges best reflects the approximate combined *annual* income of everyone in the household, *after tax?*

Please include income from all sources, including wages, government pensions and benefits and investments.

1. USD 1-USD 14 800.
2. USD 14 801-USD 22 200.
3. USD 22 201-USD 29 100.
4. USD 29 101-USD 35 200.
5. USD 35 201-USD 41 300.
6. USD 41 301-USD 47 500.
7. USD 47 501-USD 54 700.
8. USD 54 701-USD 62 900.
9. USD 62 901-USD 73 500.
10. USD 73 501-USD 91 700.
11. USD 91 701-USD 119 200.
12. More than USD 119 200.
13. Don't know.
14. Prefer not to answer.

12. Are you the person who earns the most in your household?

1. Yes.
2. No.
3. Don't know.

13. Do you and/or another member of your household own your current primary residence?

1. Yes.
2. No.

14a. Is your primary residence?

1. An apartment in a building with less than 12 apartments in total.
2. An apartment in a building with more than 12 apartments.
3. A detached house.
4. A semi-detached/terraced house.
5. Other (specify).

14b. Approximately how many months per year do you live in your current primary residence?

15. How many rooms are there in your home?

Please exclude bathrooms:

1. 1
2. 2
3. 3
4. 4
5. 5
6. 6
7. 7
8. 8
9. 9
10. 10
11. 11
12. 12 or more.

16. What is the approximate size of your primary residence in square feet? (Please estimate)

- **Residence:**
  1. Less than 270 ft^2.
  2. 270 ft^2–540 ft^2.
  3. 541 ft^2–1 070 ft^2.
  4. 1 071 ft^2–1 610 ft^2.
  5. 1 611 ft^2–2 150 ft^2.
  6. More than 2 150 ft^2.
  7. Don't know.
- **Garden/terrace/balcony:**
  1. No garden/terrace/balcony possessed.
  2. Less than 110 ft^2.
  3. 110 ft^2–540 ft^2.
  4. 541 ft^2–1 610 ft^2.
  5. 1 611 ft^2–3 230 ft^2.

6. More than 3 230 ft^2.

7. Don't know.

17. How would you best describe the area in which you live?

1. Isolated dwelling (not in a town or village).

2. Rural.

3. Suburban (fringes of a major town/city).

4. Urban.

18. Approximately how long ago was your primary residence constructed?

1. Less than 5 years ago.

2. Between 5 and 15 years ago.

3. Between 16 and 30 years ago.

4. Between 31 and 50 years ago.

5. Between 51 and 80 years ago.

6. More than 80 years ago.

7. Don't know.

19. Approximately how many years have you lived in your primary residence?

1. Less than 2 years.

2. 2 to 5 years.

3. 6 to 15 years.

4. More than 15 years.

20. What is the postal code of your primary residence?

PART B – ATTITUDINAL CHARACTERISTICS

21. Please rank the following issues in order of their importance to you.

1 stands for the most important and 6 for the least important.

Drag or double click on an issue on the left to move it to the right hand side. If you want to reorder an issue once it is on the right hand side, select it and then use the up and down arrows:

1. International tensions (terrorism, war).

2. Economic concerns (unemployment, inflation).

3. Environmental concerns (waste, air pollution).

4. Health concerns (Bird flu, AIDS).

5. Social issues (poverty, discrimination).

6. Personal safety (crime, theft…).

22. How concerned are you about the following environmental issues?

Please select one answer per row:

	Not concerned	Fairly concerned	Concerned	Very concerned	No opinion
Waste generation					
Air pollution					
Climate change (global warming)					
Water pollution					
Natural resource depletion (forest, water, energy)					
Genetically modified organisms (GMO)					
Endangered species and biodiversity					
Noise					

23. Have you voted in any of the following types of elections in the past 6 years?

Please select all that apply:

1. National/general elections.

2. Local elections.

3. None of the above.

24. In the past 24 months have you given any of your personal time to support or participate in activities of any of the following types of groups/organisations?

Please select as applies:

1. Parent-teacher association.
2. Environmental organisation.
3. Local community organisation.
4. Charitable organisation.
5. Other association/organisation.
6. None of the above.

25. Are you currently a member of, or contributor/donator to, any environmental organisations?

1. Yes.
2. No.

26. To what extent do you agree with each of the following statements?

Please select one answer per row:

	Strongly disagree	Disagree	Agree	Strongly agree	No opinion
Each individual/household can contribute to a better environment					
Environmental impacts are frequently overstated					
Environmental issues should be dealt with primarily by future generations					
Environmental issues will be resolved primarily through technological progress					
Environmental policies introduced by the government to address environmental issues should not cost me extra money					

27. Please rank the following sources of information on environmental issues in terms of their trustworthiness.

1 stands for the most trustworthy and 5 for the least trustworthy:

1. Independent researchers and experts.
2. National/Local governments.

3. Environmental non-governmental organisations (NGOs).

4. Consumers' organisations.

5. Producers' and retailers' associations.

28. For each of the following categories, how often does your household choose to use the products listed, rather than the alternatives?

Please select one answer per row:

	Never	Occasionally	Often	Always	Don't know
Paper with recycled content (*e.g.* stationery)					
Products with reduced toxic content (*e.g.* environmentally friendly cleaning products)					
Refillable containers (*e.g.* bottles, washing detergents)					
Reusable shopping bags					

29. Which factors discourage you from buying?

Please select all that apply:

1. Product availability.

2. Product quality (*e.g.* considered inferior).

3. Product appearance (*e.g.* colour, packaging).

4. Price (too expensive).

5. Not familiar with the product(s).

6. Not interested.

30. Among the following logos/labels, please select the ones you are familiar with:

[An image is shown to the respondents].

❐ None of the above.

31. Among the following logos/labels, select the ones you take into account in your purchasing decisions:

PART C – WASTE

The following section will cover waste generation and recycling.

32. How often is your household mixed waste collected (by a third party) from your primary residence or from containers where you dispose of your waste?

This excludes waste sorted for recycling/composting:

1. More than once a week.

2. Once a week.

3. Less than once a week.

4. Don't know.

33. On average, how much mixed waste does your household put out for collection *each week*?

Please indicate the approximate number of bags, taking the size of the bags in the picture below as a reference:

[An image is shown to the respondents].

Mixed waste for collection	Number of bags

1. None.

2. 1

3. 2

4. 3

5. 4

6. 5

7. 6

8. 7

9. 8

10. 9

11. 10

12. 11

13. 12

14. 13

15. 14 or more.

16. Don't know.

34. What are the waste collection services available for recyclable materials in your area?

Select all that apply:

	Door-to-door collection	Drop-off centres/ containers	Bring back with refund (to the retailer/ manufacturer)	Bring back with no refund (to the retailer/ manufacturer)	No service available	Don't know
Glass bottles/containers						
Plastic bottles/containers						
Aluminium, tin and steel cans						
Paper/cardboard						
Food or garden waste						

35. How often are X collected door to door?

1. More than once a week.

2. Once a week.

3. Less than once a week.

4. Don't know.

36. Which of the following materials does your household recycle?

1. Glass bottles/containers.

2. Plastic bottles/containers.

3. Aluminium, tin and steel cans.

4. Paper/cardboard.

5. Food waste.

6. Garden waste.

7. Batteries (domestic).

8. Pharmaceuticals/medicines.

9. None of the above.

37. Please indicate approximately what percentage of the materials above your household recycles?

It includes returns to the retailer/manufacturer:

1. 25%.

2. 50%.

3. 75%.

4. 100%.

5. Don't know.

38. How important are the following factors in motivating your household to recycle?

Please select one answer per row:

	Not at all important	Not important	Fairly important	Very important	Not applicable
It is beneficial for the environment					
It is mandated by the government					
I want to save/receive money					
I think it is my civic duty					
I want to be seen by others as a responsible citizen					

39. Approximately how many minutes does your household spend on average *each week* on recycling activities?

Time spent to (clean) sort and store your recyclable waste as well as bring it to drop-off containers/centres or door-to-door collection:

1. Less than 5 minutes.
2. 5 to 14 minutes.
3. 15 to 29 minutes.
4. 30 to 59 minutes.
5. 1 to 2 hours.
6. More than 2 hours.
7. Don't know.

40a. How important would the following factors be in encouraging your household to start recycling?

Please select one answer per row:

	Not at all important	Not very important	Quite important	Very important
More practical information on how to recycle (what is recyclable, services available, etc.)				
Greater financial incentives (saving/receiving money)				
More storage space at home				
Having more time to recycle				
Improved collection and recycling services (more frequent, more accessible)				
Stronger belief that the environmental benefits are significant				

❏ None of the above would encourage my household to start recycling.

40b. How important would the following factors be in encouraging your household to recycle more?

	Not at all important	Not very important	Quite important	Very important
More practical information on how to recycle (what is recyclable, services available, etc.)				
Greater financial incentives (saving/receiving money)				
More storage space at home				
Having more time to recycle				
Improved collection and recycling services (more frequent, more accessible)				
Stronger belief that the environmental benefits are significant				

❐ None of the above would encourage my household to recycle more.

41. If the current system were to be changed in such a way that you need not separate your waste at home at all, but this is done on your behalf by a third party, how much would you be willing to pay *each month* for this service?

Please select one:

1. USD 0.
2. USD 1.
3. USD 2.
4. USD 3.
5. USD 4.
6. USD 5.
7. USD 6.
8. USD 7.
9. USD 8.
10. USD 9.
11. USD 10.
12. USD 11.
13. USD 12.
14. USD 13.
15. USD 14.
16. USD 15.
17. USD 16.

18. USD 17.

19. USD 18.

20. USD 19.

21. USD 20.

22. USD 21.

23. USD 22.

24. USD 23.

25. USD 24.

26. USD 25

27. USD 26

28. USD 27

29. USD 28

30. USD 29.

31. USD 30 or more.

32. Don't know.

42. Why would you not be willing to pay anything?

1. Prefer to be responsible for recycling.

2. Cannot afford it.

3. It does not concern me.

4. Other, please specify:

43. How would you characterise the issue of illegal dumping* in your area?

Please select one:

1. Not an issue.

2. Minor problem.

3. Moderately important problem.

4. Major problem.

5. Don't know.

* By illegal dumping we mean the disposal of household waste in a non-permitted area.

44. How do you think illegal dumping* could be more effectively controlled?

Please select all that apply:

1. Regulation against illegal dumping should be better enforced (including fines).
2. Waste collection services should better meet household demand (availability, accessibility).
3. Information on available waste disposal services should be increased.
4. Charges for collection and management of waste should be lower.
5. No opinion.

45. How is your household charged for the collection and management of mixed waste in your primary residence?

Please select one:

1. Flat fee (*e.g.* lump sum included in property taxes, charges or rent).
2. Volume-based unit charge/price (per bag, container, etc.).
3. Weight-based unit charge/price (per kg, pound, etc.).
4. Frequency based charge (according to how often the waste is collected).
5. Charge/price based on household size.
6. Other form of charging, please specify:
7. Not charged.
8. Don't know.

---

* By illegal dumping we mean the disposal of household waste in a non-permitted area.

PART D – TRANSPORT

The following section will cover personal transport.

In this section, when using the word "car" we also include vans and sport utility vehicles (SUV).

46. How many vehicles are owned or used regularly by your household (including company cars)?

Number of car(s):

1. 0
2. 1
3. 2
4. 3
5. 4
6. 5 or more.

Number of motorcycle(s):

1. 0
2. 1
3. 2
4. 3
5. 4
6. 5 or more.

47. What is the main reason for your household not having a car?

Please select one:

1. Can't afford a car.
2. Can get everywhere we want without a car.
3. No one can/wants drive.
4. Environmental concerns.
5. Other, please specify:

48. Please enter the information concerning the car you use most often.

	Fuel type	Age of the car (years)	Seating capacity (persons)	Engine size
Car used most often				

Fuel Type:

1. Unleaded.
2. Leaded.
3. LPG (liquefied petroleum gas).
4. Diesel.
5. Hybrid.
6. Biofuels.
7. Electric.
8. Don't know.

Age of the car:

1. Less than 1 year old.
2. 1 year old.
3. 2 years old.
4. 3 years old.
5. 4 years old.
6. 5 years old.
7. 6 years old.
8. 7 years old.
9. 8 years old.
10. 9 years old.
11. 10 years old.
12. 11 years old.
13. 12 years old.
14. 13 years old.
15. 14 years old.
16. 15 years old.
17. 16 years old.
18. 17 years old.

19. 18 years old.

20. 19 years old.

21. 20 years old.

22. 21 years old.

23. 22 years old.

24. 23 years old.

25. 24 years old.

26. 25 years old or older.

27. Don't know.

Seating capacity:

1. 1 person.

2. 2 people.

3. 3 people.

4. 4 people.

5. 5 people.

6. 6 people.

7. 7 people.

8. 8 people.

9. More than 8 people.

Engine size:

1. Less than 1 litre.

2. 1- 1.5 litres.

3. 1.6-2 litres.

4. 2.1-3 litres.

5. More than 3 litres.

6. Don't know.

49. How far is your primary residence from the public transport stop/station which is most convenient for your daily commute?

Please select the corresponding means of transport usually used to get there (walking, driving, public transport) and indicate the time required in minutes:

Usual means of transport	Average time in minutes (one way)	Don't know	No public transport stop/station available	Not applicable
Walking	Less than 5 minutes			
Car/motorcycle	5 to 15			
Public transport	16 to 30			
Bicycle	31 to 45			
	46 minutes to 1 hour			
	More than 1 hour			

50. How many kilometres do you personally drive (car/motorcycle) during a typical *week*?

1. Do not drive.
2. Less than 30 km.
3. 31-100 km.
4. 101-250 km.
5. 251-500 km.
6. 501-700 km.
7. 701-900 km.
8. 901 km-1 000 km.
9. More than 1 001 km.
10. Don't know.

51. What would encourage you to drive (car/motorcycle) less?

Select all that apply:

1. Increased cost of car/motorcycle use.
2. Better public transport.
3. Cheaper public transport.
4. More and safer cycling paths.
5. Other (please specify):
6. None of the above would make me use a car/motorcycle less.

52. What aspects of public transport are likely to encourage you to use your car/motorcycle less?

	Not at all likely	Not very likely	Quite likely	Very likely
More convenient (*e.g.* stops closer to home and destination)				
More reliable (*e.g.* fewer delays, strikes)				
More rapid (*e.g.* higher frequency, speed)				
More comfortable (*e.g.* less crowded)				
More secure (*e.g.* improved personal safety)				

53. What would be the likely effect of a permanent increase in fuel prices of 20% on your fuel consumption for your personal car/motorcycle use? (E.g. by driving less, buying a more fuel efficient vehicle, etc.)

Please select one:

1. Would not change.

2. Would reduce by less than 10%.

3. Would reduce by between 10% and 20%.

4. Would reduce by more than 20%.

5. Don't know.

6. Prefer not to answer.

54. What is your main mode of transportation for each of the following activities?

If you use a combination of modes for a given activity please select more than one answer per row:

	Walking	Car	Public transport	Bicycle	Motorcycle	Not applicable
Daily commute to and from work						
Travel undertaken for your usual professional activities						
Visiting family and friends (excluding vacation/week-end trips)						
Shopping						
Education						
Sports and cultural activities						

55. Approximately how long does it take you to get to work (one way)?

1. Less than 15 min.
2. 15-30 min.
3. 31-45 min.
4. 46 min-1 hour.
5. More than 1 hour.

56. For the following travel purposes, how long does it take you to use public transport compared to driving a car or a motorcycle (one way)?

When applicable please select one answer per row:

	Less time					Same time	More time					Not possible	Don't know
	−60 min	−46 to 60 min	−31 to 45 min	−16 to 30 min	−5 to 15 min		+5 to 15 min	+16 to 30 min	+31 to 45 min	+46 to 60 min	+60 min		
Daily commute to and from work													
Travel undertaken for your usual professional activities													
Shopping													
Education													

57. What are the approximate costs associated with your own travel each *month* for the following?

Please fill in as appropriate and provide your answer to the nearest dollar:

	Amount in USD per month	Not applicable	Don't know
Fuel			
Parking			
Charges for road usage (*e.g.* road/city tolls)			
Public transport			

58. During the past year, have you done any of the following?

Select all that apply:

1. Used car sharing/pooling.
2. Used recycled tires/low rolling resistance tires.
3. Offset your carbon emissions.
4. Changed a car for another one which uses less fuel.
5. Used public transport more than the previous year.
6. Walked or cycled more than the previous year.
7. Adapted your driving style to use less fuel (*e.g.* reduce speed, reduce air conditioning use).
8. Changed a car for another one which uses less polluting fuel.
9. None of the above.

PART E – ENERGY

The following section will cover residential energy use.

59. Which of the following sources of energy do you use in your primary residence?

Select all that apply:

1. Electricity.
2. Natural gas.
3. Fuel oil.
4. Wood or wood chips.
5. Coal.
6. District heating.
7. Other (please specify):

60. In your household, which of the bills do you pay according to your household consumption?

Select all that apply:

1. Electricity.
2. Natural gas.
3. Fuel oil.
4. Wood or wood chips.
5. Coal.
6. District heating.
7. Other option selected in 59.
8. None of the above.

61. Does the electricity price paid by your household vary according to the time of use?

This would imply that your household would pay a lower price during off-peak period (e.g. night time) and a higher price during peak period (e.g. early evening):

1. Yes.
2. No.
3. Don't know.

62. Does your household take special measures to buy *renewable energy* from your *electricity provider?*

By renewable energy we mean energy sources such as wind, solar, geothermal, hydro:

1. Yes.
2. No.
3. Don't know.

63. Please state why you do not buy renewable energy:

1. Service not available and our household is not interested.
2. Service not available, but our household would be interested to do so.
3. Service available, but our household is not interested.
4. Energy from electricity provider is already from renewable energy sources.
5. I don't know anything about these kinds of services.

64. What is the maximum percentage increase on your annual bill that you are willing to pay to use *only renewable energy?*

Please assume that your energy consumption remains constant:

1. I would not pay anything additional.
2. Less than 5%.
3. 5%-15%.
4. 16%-30%.
5. More than 30%.
6. Don't know.

65. Did you take energy costs into account when purchasing or renting your current primary residence?

1. Yes.
2. No.
3. Not sure.

66. Which of the following appliances do you have in your primary residence?

1. Dishwashers.
2. Clothes washers/clothes washer-dryers.
3. Clothes dryers.
4. Fridges/fridge-freezers.

5. Separate freezers.

6. Ovens.

7. Microwave ovens.

8. Electric water heating boilers.

9. Televisions.

10. Set-top boxes.

11. Computers.

12. Air conditioners.

67. How many of the following appliances do you have?

1. Fridges.

2. Separate freezers.

3. Televisions.

4. Set-top boxes.

5. Computers.

6. Air conditioners:

    a) 1

    b) 2

    c) 3

    d) 4

    e) 5 or more.

68. How often do you perform the following in your daily life?

Please select one answer per row:

	Never	Occasionally	Often	Always
Turn off lights when leaving a room				
Cut down on heating/air conditioning to limit your energy consumption				
Wait until you have full loads when using washing machines or dishwashers				
Turn off appliances when not in use				
Switch off standby mode of appliances/electronic devices				

69. Has your household installed any of the following items over the past ten years in your current primary residence?

If these measures are not feasible in your house/apartment or if they would need to be carried out by the landlord, select "not possible".

	Yes	No	Already equipped	Not possible
Energy-efficiency-rated appliances (*e.g.* top rated washing machines, refrigerators)				
Low-energy light bulbs (compact fluorescent)				
Thermal insulation (*e.g.* walls/roof insulation, double-glazing)				
Efficient heating boiler (*e.g.* condensing boiler)				
Renewable energy (*e.g.* to install solar panels, wind turbines)				

70. For which of the following has your household benefited from support from the government (for instance grants, preferential loans, energy audits)?

For which of the items above has your household benefited from support from... energy audits)?

❒ None of the above.

71. How important are the following factors in encouraging you to reduce your energy consumption?

	Not at all important	Not important	Fairly important	Very Important
More practical information on energy conservation measures[1]				
Higher energy prices				
Belief that the environmental benefits are significant				
Greater availability of energy-efficient products				
Easier identification of energy efficiency labels				
Less expensive to invest in energy-efficient equipment				

1. By energy conservation measures we mean for instance investments in energy efficient equipment (fridge), thermal insulation.

PART F – ORGANIC FOOD

The following section will cover organic food consumption.

By organic we mean a production process where, depending on the standard, fewer chemicals (i.e. pesticides, fertilisers, drugs, additives), if any, are used.

72. Do you have primary (or shared) responsibility for food shopping in the household?

1. Yes.

2. No.

73. Please estimate your household's average *weekly* expenditures on *food* for the following items.

Please do not include expenditures in restaurants or canteens:

	Amount in USD per week *Please provide your answer to the nearest dollar*	Don't know	Not applicable/product not consumed in the household
Fresh fruits and vegetables			
Milk and other dairy products			
Eggs			
Meat and poultry			
Bread, pasta, rice and cereal			

74. Please estimate the percentage of expenditures of your household for the following items which are *organic products.*

Please select one answer per row:

	0%	1%- 5%	6%- 10%	11%- 25%	26%- 50%	51%- 75%	76%- 99%	100%	Consume organic products but % unknown	Don't know if consume organic products at all
Fresh fruits and vegetables										
Milk and other dairy products										
Eggs										
Meat and poultry										
Bread, pasta, rice and cereal										

75. Please rank the following factors in terms of the importance of their effect on your motivation to consume (or buy) organic food?

1 stands for the most important and 5 for the least important:

1. Respect animal welfare.
2. Better for health.
3. Better taste.
4. Support small and local farmers.
5. Preserve the environment.

76. What is the maximum percentage price increase you are willing to pay for organic products of the following categories compared to conventional substitutes?

	0%	1-5%	6-15%	16-30%	31-50%	> 50%	Don't know
Fresh fruits and vegetables							
Milk and other dairy products							
Eggs							
Meat and poultry							
Bread, pasta, rice and cereal							

77. What would encourage you to start consuming (to consume more) organic food products?

Please select one answer per row:

	Not at all important	Not important	Fairly important	Very important
Better availability of organic products				
Lower price of organic products				
Better appearance of the food				
More trust in health benefits of organic products				
More trust in environmental benefits of organic products				
More trust in certification and labelling of organic products				

❒ None of the above.

78. Would you continue to consume (start to consume) – or buy – organic food if it was found that:

Please give one answer per row:

	Yes	No	Don't know
Organic food is better for the environment, but no indication that it is better for personal health			
Organic food is better for personal health, but no indication that it is better for the environment			

79. In your opinion, how easy is it to identify organic food labels/logos when buying products?

1. Very difficult.
2. Quite difficult.
3. Quite easy.
4. Very easy.
5. No opinion.

80. In your opinion, how understandable are organic food labels/logos?

1. Very difficult to understand.
2. Fairly difficult to understand.
3. Fairly easy to understand.
4. Very easy to understand.
5. No opinion.

PART G – WATER

The following section will cover water consumption and use.

81. Is your household charged for water consumption in your primary residence?

1. Yes.

2. No.

3. Not sure.

82. What would best describe your situation in your primary residence?

1. Not connected to the mains water (using a well/bore, a rainwater tank).

2. Connected to the mains water but not charged for water consumption.

3. Don't know

83. How is your household charged for water consumption?

1. Charged according to how much water is used (*e.g.* via a water meter).

2. Flat fee (*e.g.* lump sum included in charges or rent).

3. Don't know.

84. Approximately how much was the total *annual* cost for water consumption for your primary residence?

Please indicate if possible amount in USD and corresponding annual consumption in m^3:

Amount in USD per year *Please provide answer to the nearest dollar*	Volume of water consumed in m^3

❐ Don't know.

85. How often do you do the following in your daily life?

Please select one answer per row:

	Never	Occasionally	Often	Always	Not applicable
Turn off the water while brushing teeth					
Take showers instead of bath specifically to save water					
Plug the sink when washing the dishes					
Water your garden in the coolest part of the day to reduce evaporation and save water					
Collect rainwater (*e.g.* in water tanks) or recycle waste water					

86. Has your household invested in the following appliances/devices in the past 10 years in your current primary residence?

If these measures would need to be carried out by the landlord, select "Not possible".

	Yes	No	Already equipped	Not possible
Water efficient washing machines				
Low volume or dual flush toilets				
Water flow restrictor taps/low flow shower head				
Water tank to collect rainwater				
Water purifier for drinking water				

87. For which of the following has your household benefited from government support to make this investment (for instance grants and incentives)?

Please select all that apply:

1. Filter items 1-4 selected in the "yes" column in Q92.

2. Don't know.

3. None of the above.

88. How important are the following factors in encouraging you to reduce your water consumption?

	Not at all important	Not important	Fairly important	Very important
Practical information on things you can do to save water at home				
Money savings				
Clear importance of the environmental benefits of saving water				
Availability of water-efficient products				
Confidence in water-efficiency labels				
Lower cost of water-efficient equipment				
Mandatory water restrictions (*e.g.* periodic bans on watering garden)				
None of the above				

89. Do you drink tap water for your normal household consumption?

1. Yes.
2. No.

90. Are you satisfied with the quality of your tap water for drinking?

1. Yes.
2. No.

91. In your tap water, what is of most concern to you?

1. Taste.
2. Concern about health impacts.
3. Neither of these.

92. What is the maximum percentage increase you would be willing to pay above your actual water bill to improve the quality of your tap water, holding water consumption constant?

1. Nothing.
2. Less than 5%.
3. Between 5% and 15%.
4. Between 16% and 30%.
5. More than 30%.
6. Don't know.

ANNEX C

Research Teams Involved in the 2008 OECD Household Survey Data Analysis

The project was co-ordinated by the Empirical Policy Analysis Unit of the OECD Environment Directorate, with research teams with extensive experience based in selected participating countries. These include:*

1. **Catholic University, Piacenza, Italy.** Stefano Boccaletti (research team leader): Organic food.
2. **Charles University, Prague, the Czech Republic.** Milan Ščasný (research team leader): Energy efficiency.
3. **Korean Environment Institute (KEI), Korea.** Kwang-yim Kim (research team leader): Waste generation.
4. **SLU University, Sweden.** Bengt Kriström (research team leader): Renewable energy.
5. **Statistics Norway, Norway.** Bente Halvorsen (research team leader): Gender issues.
6. **The Australian National University, Australia.** Quentin Grafton (research team leader): Water consumption.
7. **Universidad Iberoamericana, Mexico.** Alejandro Guevara-Sangines (research team leader): Transport.
8. **CNRS, University Panthéon-Sorbonne and Toulouse School of Economics and Institut National de la Recherche Agronomique (INRA), France.** Katrin Millock and Céline Nauges (research team leaders): Water conservation and water quality.
9. **York University, Canada.** Ida Ferrara (research team leader): Waste recycling and waste prevention.

* In addition to the teams listed below, invaluable inputs in data preparation and analysis were provided by Fleur Watson (OECD Secretariat), Clotilde Bureau and Renan Devillières (both formerly ENSAE – Malakoff, France).

ANNEX D

Key Policy Issues Examined

Important policy questions examined in the survey in the five areas covered include the following:

Residential energy use

- *How do general attitudes towards the environment (environmental awareness; membership of an environmental organisation;...) influence demand for energy efficiency and for renewable energy?*
- *How effective is energy efficiency labelling?*
- *Who invests in energy efficiency measures and in renewable energy?*
- *How much are households willing to pay to use only renewable energy? Does WTP vary significantly across household groups?*

Waste generation and recycling and prevention

- *Whether unit-based waste fees have significant effects on waste generation relative to "flat" (or no) fees?*
- *How do general attitudes towards the environment influence waste generation and waste recycling levels?*
- *To which extent do household waste recycling decisions depend on services provided (e.g. door-to-door collection or drop off)?*

Personal transport choices

- *How is household car use influenced by the presence of adequate public transport options?*
- *What characteristics of public transport (reliability, proximity, security, etc.) are most important in encouraging households to switch from car use?*
- *Who is the most reluctant to switch from car use?*
- *How do general attitudes towards the environment influence car use and public transport use?*

Organic food consumption

- *What encourages consumption of organic foods more – concern for private health or public environmental concerns?*
- *How effective is organic food labelling?*
- *What would households generally be willing-to-pay as a price premium to purchase organic foods?*

Environmental policies related to residential water use

- *Is there a significant difference in water consumption and investment in water efficient equipment between households which face unit water charges and those which do not?*
- *How do general attitudes towards the environment influence residential water use levels and water conservation behaviour?*
- *Who would be most adversely affected by increases in water charges?*
- *How much are households willing to pay for improved water quality?*

ORGANISATION FOR ECONOMIC CO-OPERATION AND DEVELOPMENT

The OECD is a unique forum where governments work together to address the economic, social and environmental challenges of globalisation. The OECD is also at the forefront of efforts to understand and to help governments respond to new developments and concerns, such as corporate governance, the information economy and the challenges of an ageing population. The Organisation provides a setting where governments can compare policy experiences, seek answers to common problems, identify good practice and work to co-ordinate domestic and international policies.

The OECD member countries are: Australia, Austria, Belgium, Canada, Chile, the Czech Republic, Denmark, Estonia, Finland, France, Germany, Greece, Hungary, Iceland, Ireland, Israel, Italy, Japan, Korea, Luxembourg, Mexico, the Netherlands, New Zealand, Norway, Poland, Portugal, the Slovak Republic, Slovenia, Spain, Sweden, Switzerland, Turkey, the United Kingdom and the United States. The European Commission takes part in the work of the OECD.

OECD Publishing disseminates widely the results of the Organisation's statistics gathering and research on economic, social and environmental issues, as well as the conventions, guidelines and standards agreed by its members.

OECD PUBLISHING, 2, rue André-Pascal, 75775 PARIS CEDEX 16
(97 2010 14 1 P) ISBN 978-92-64-06362-4 – No. 57809 2011